"I love that Ryan has always approached personal branding from a practical level. The DICE process isn't academic or theoretical, it's usable and effective from the get-go. Taking the time to understand how to clearly communicate who you are and the value you provide on a professional level is an investment that will pay you back over and over. Read this book. Do the work. I promise you'll love the results."

David J.P. Fisher
Author of Hyper-Connected Selling and Networking in the 21st Century

"I had the age-old issue of "I know what I do, but I don't really know how to talk about it very well or how to describe it." After only one hour of MY time, Ryan was able to do for me what I have not been able to do myself over the last 12 months: clearly and succinctly describe my unique work process. Because of Ryan, I now have the tools to build a killer website, develop a consistent blog, describe what I do in 3 easy steps, and brand and market my unique leadership/team development process."

Claudia Williams
Founder & Chief Frientorship™ Officer, The Human Zone LLC

"Ryan's system takes an overwhelming topic and breaks it down into an easy to understand system that works. His guidance has been invaluable in building my own brand"

Shane Purnell
Speaker, Founder of Platform Giant Communication

"Ryan is a true expert on personal branding. Using his DICE process, I have elevated my CareerKred by first figuring out what I wanted to be know for, then making that thing known to the world and finally engaging with others to demonstrate my expertise in that area. His book is chock-full of both principles and specific actions for establishing your brand online. I highly recommend this book to anyone looking to stand out in their career."

Brandon Heavey
Founder, Evidence Based Athlete

"Ryan has spent years researching personal brands and it shows! This book is packed with actionable tips to create your online personal brand. Ryan's simple four step DICE process opened my eyes to how much I am lacking when it comes to developing my personal brand. By following the four step process, I was able to make strides on how I am perceived online. If you plan to succeed in your career, this book is for you."

Dustin Hartzler
Founder, YourWebsiteEngineer.com

"Ryan is one of the most brilliant people I know. Using his online assessment and DICE process, Ryan was able to quickly identify the weak spots in my online persona and build a framework that would become my new brand: Me. Ryan helped me position myself as a subject matter expert and overcome a serious case of imposter syndrome."

Steve Stewart
Owner, stevestewart.me

"It isn't enough to do your job well and expect a promotion. Nor can you just bundle your skills, traits and expertise and label this your brand. You need career credibility and Ryan Rhoten's CareerKred. Rhoten is living proof that you can build career credibility. It starts by developing your brand and integrating it online by creating content and engaging with people. This worked for Rhoten and it can work for you too. Rhoten's D.I.C.E. process maps out the steps you must take to expand your reputation—online and in-person. Your career success rests solely in your hands so allow Rhoten to expertly walk you through exactly what you need to do to propel your career and ensure a future pipeline of opportunities."

Hannah Morgan, Job Search Strategist
Founder, CareerSherpa.net

"Ryan is a personal branding force to be reckoned with. He weaves digital branding know-how with honest and compelling storytelling. The DICE process takes an often nebulous "personal branding" concept and breaks it down into actionable and attainable steps—it is an indispensable strategy for anyone looking to take their career to the next level."

Sabrina Clark
Marketing Director, Brandyourself.com

"After reading Ryan's book, it confirmed several things for me:

- Stop thinking obtusely about your career and start taking control of your personal brand
- An assessment is only as good as the actions taken afterward
- An unmonitored personal brand is equal to letting go of the wheel driving around a curve

Ryan's book will force you to rethink your career trajectory, forget any previous strategies that include coasting or settling, and master your destiny (even when it incessantly shifts). Mastering your CareerKred will change the expectations of what your career might be, and help you control your career to what it should be. If you're tempted to automate your career, stop! Consider how CareerKred will power-up your personal branding efforts online and have future business partners, employers, and/or clients find you."

Mark Anthony Dyson

CareerKred

Four Simple Steps to Build Your Digital Brand and Boost Credibility in Your Career

Ryan Rhoten

Publishedby
CareerBrand Publishing
601 - 16th Street #339
Golden, CO 80401

Manufactured in the United States of America, or in the United Kingdom when distributed elsewhere.

Rhoten, Ryan
CareerKred

ISBN:
Paperback: 978-1-7324935-0-6
eBook: 978-1-7324935-1-3

Cover design by: Debbie O'Byrne

www.ryanrhoten.com

Impacting your career through your digital brand shouldn't be so hard. By following the 4 simple steps of the DICE process you can get found and recognized for your expertise. If you're looking to boost your credibility, CareerKred is a must read even if you don't know where to start.

Table of Contents

Part Four: The Integrate Step

Part Five: The Create Step

Part Six: The Engage Step

Foreword

When I first connected with Ryan on social media, he immediately stood out. His personal brand was powerful and personable. Despite the fact we were on opposite sides of the world, his personality resonated and shone through his online presence. I think this is the greatest challenge we face when it comes to our personal branding: we can easily forget just how much of a personable connection we can still make in this digital-first world.

Years ago, your personal brand was "your promise to the world", as stated by US business author Tom Peters in *Forbes* magazine. This was back in 1997. Today, things are different. Your personal brand is more than face-to-face communication, and it's more than interaction through an in-person connection. In today's world of noise, technology and digital connection, how we are *perceived* is integral to our personal brand. It's critical to the amount of influence we have and our ability to build trust with our clients and the people we want to work with.

Another great challenge we face, particularly in Australia, is the "tall poppy syndrome". This is where it's not cool to stand out. It's not cool to draw attention to ourselves or look like a know-it-all. But to make an impact, we must stand out. This is because job markets are changing. By 2020, 50% of the workforce will be self-employed. The "career for life" no longer exists. More than ever, our personal brand matters so that we can create our own job security, career and business success. Because, at the end of the day, people buy from people, and they buy from people who they know, like and trust.

I know this from personal experience. I started a business with a brand that was not my own name, and I quickly became commoditised.

I found myself competing on price, which is an incredibly challenging space to be in. But when I changed the brand of the business to my name, everything changed immediately. People took me more seriously. I had more influence and I built greater trust with my clients.

Your online presence matters. Research tells us that it takes 10 pieces of content for somebody to want to work with you. In fact, 90% of their decision is now made before they even get in touch with you. Our customer journeys have changed dramatically; the phone book simply doesn't exist anymore.

But when you connect with somebody like Ryan, what immediately stands out is his ability to solve problems. And, essentially, that's what a personal brand is: your ability to build a deep connection and demonstrate to clients how you can solve their problems. That way, you repel the people who are not your ideal clients and attract those who are.

Ryan's education and skills perfectly position him to diagnose and solve customer problems. He has not only completed his MBA, he has also studied aeronautical technology. He is customer-focused and customer-centric, with a keen ability to detect and resolve underlying issues.

Ryan has also achieved some incredible feats: his Twitter account is a must-follow for people who are trying to improve their job search. He has HubSpot email and content marketing certification, which is enormously valuable for clients who are trying to get cut-through with their communication. He's also at the leading edge of what personal branding means in the digital and human economy. His podcast, The Brand New You Show, has achieved an incredible number of downloads.

Ryan's DICE technique is such a simple yet powerful way for people to grow their positioning, persuasion and personal connection with clients. His diagnostic helps people measure the effectiveness of their personal brand, so they can self-diagnose exactly what gaps they need to fill.

His real strength lies in his ability to break down complex challenges. With more than 20 years' experience in customer-value chains, Ryan can help people work through seemingly insurmountable challenges so they can achieve what they want to achieve with their personal brand. He supports people to implement real change so they can access their ideal clients, create powerful communication and cut-through, and grow their businesses.

In this great book Ryan has written, *CareerKred*, you'll have access to Ryan's digital brand assessment. It includes key activities that are super practical and can be applied to your own personal brand. You'll be able to build greater trust, differentiate yourself through your expertise, and create powerful communication that amplifies your credibility.

Take advantage of every word that Ryan has written in his fantastic book, *CareerKred*. You'll learn how to stand out from the crowd without feeling cocky or arrogant. You'll be able to connect, engage, inspire and transform your business. And you'll create security for yourself, working with your ideal clients, being paid what you're worth and having a greater impact on the planet.

JANE ANDERSON
e: jane@jane-anderson.com.au
m: 0401 464 130 t: 07 3841 7772
www.janeandersonspeaks.com

Acknowledgments

To be honest, this is a section of every book I've always skimmed, if not passed over completely. As a reader, I knew the Acknowledgments page was important, but now as an author, I realize its true significance. Acknowledgments stand as a signal that no good work can be done in a vacuum and all great works come via teamwork.

With that in mind, the team who contributed to this book are all vastly smarter than I am. I just had the fortunate pleasure to meet them using the methods taught in this book. My hope is that this section will help you understand how building and maintaining a network of like-minded friends, whether in-person or virtual, can impact your life's path as well as your career.

If I tried to name every person who contributed in some way to the creation of this book, it would become a book itself, so I will spare you the complete list. For those who have contributed whether directly or indirectly, I want to thank you from the bottom of my heart. Your gifts of knowledge, wisdom, kindness, and graciousness will not be forgotten. You know who you are.

Thank you to all my podcasts guests. Many of you put your faith in a podcasting newbie, and for that I will be forever grateful. Thank you for placing more value on getting your message out to assist more people than on statistics like downloads or subscribers.

Thank you to my mastermind partners, Dustin Hartzler, Steve Stewart, Joseph Michael Nicoletti, Brandon Heavey, Michael Faron, and Dr. Ryan Gray. Your sometimes-brutal honesty has not only shaped my business, but it has also helped shape who I've become. I know, it's taken me awhile, but I'm starting to get it.

To those specifically mentioned in this book, Mark Babbitt, Madalyn Sklar, Dorie Clark, Shane Purnell, Katrina Collier, Maria Elena

Duron, Claudia Altucher, Richard Kirby, Hannah Morgan, Don Orlando, Trevor Young, Sabrina Clark, Jane Anderson, Kylie Chown, Taylor Pearson, Michelle Robins, Todd Lohenry, Marc Miller, Mark Anthony Dyson, Lisa Cummings, Matthew Capala, and Tim Saumier, thank you one and all. Your experiences, insights, and graciousness have challenged me and helped me form many of the principles discussed in this book.

Toi Sweeney and David Fisher, thank you both for your tweets, texts, and words of encouragement throughout this process. Writing a book is hard, and you two made it much easier.

To my parents, Ron and Mary, or as they are better known Oma and Opa, thank you for always being there and for pushing me to be the best husband, father, brother and person I can be.

Opa, while your time here was too short and I know you will never read this, thank you for always challenging me to think bigger and for setting the example to always serve others first. You were a true Relentless Giver.

Kate Rhoten, I often joke that I saved you, but in reality it is the other way around. Your love, support, and ability to put up with my free spirit, idiosyncrasies, and "experiments" over the years more than anything else has allowed me to become the person, husband, and father I am today. Even if I don't have a drone.

Finally, to my boys, Noah and Seth, I have tried to show you by example over the years that you do not need to follow the conventional career path. Instead you can make your own. This book is my example of the nontraditional path as well as the road map you can use to get there—even though it is over one hundred pages. I love you both more than you will ever know. Forever and Always, Dad.

Part One

Introduction

"The best way to predict the future is to create it."
—Abraham Lincoln

Chapter 1

Backstory

It was a Friday. It seems it always happens on a Friday. I had interviewed for the position a month ago and had been waiting to find out the verdict. It feels like that, doesn't it? More like a verdict from a judge than a decision from a senior leader.

The call came around three o'clock in the afternoon. "Can you come to my office?" I heard through the phone.

"I'll be right there," I responded. I mean, what else was I going to say? This was, after all, the news I had been waiting for the last five years. I'd put in my time, and now it was my time; I'd earned it. I jumped out of my chair and headed toward his office.

I was confident that this was it. In addition to all my hard work, I was next in line for this promotion. My peers knew it, too, and they all agreed that I was the person for the job. It wasn't just my peers, either; my boss agreed as well. He had told me so just that morning.

All my hard work was about to pay off in the form a promotion, a title, and a door. The corporate office equivalent of the trifecta, the hat trick, or a turkey (a turkey is three strikes in a row in bowling).

Even though he was expecting me, I knocked on the door to his office before I walked in. "Ryan, come on in; sit down," he said with a smile, but I could tell by the look on his face that something was not quite right. But I couldn't be 100 percent sure. After all, he had started with the company only three months ago, and my exposure to him had been limited almost solely to our interview.

He had come from the outside to fill a senior level position left vacant by a restructuring. In all honesty, a lot of people, including myself, thought the position should have been given to an internal candidate who had been in his role for several years. This seemed like the natural progression to many of us, but it was not to be.

I hadn't even fully settled into the chair when I heard him say, "Ryan, I'm going to cut to the chase. You didn't get the position." He went on for a few more minutes, explaining how the company was evolving, taking a new direction, yada yada yada, but I didn't hear a word. I just stared at him, dumbfounded.

That was how I found myself smack in the middle of a career crisis.

I had no idea how I got there. I had done everything they had asked of me and more. I had twenty-plus years of experience, eight of which had been with this very company. I had learned the ins and outs of the industry, attended trade shows, held customer meetings, negotiated supplier agreements, and built an entire organization from the ground up. Yet here I was on the drive home that Friday afternoon with only one thought in my mind.

I got passed over.

To say I was devastated would be an understatement. I was at a loss for words, and even worse, no one offered to help. The following Monday I scheduled a meeting with the hiring manager to try to understand why I didn't get the job. What was the skill I was missing, the knowledge I needed to obtain, etc.? Without going into detail, the meeting ended with the comment, "It could have been you."

But it wasn't, and no one could tell me why. Not the hiring manager, not human resources, not even my peers. No one offered any help. I was left alone with my thoughts. I felt totally dejected, and I finally understood what it meant to be a disengaged employee.

At the time I had an hour-long commute to and from work. This provided me with ample time to think about my situation. As I contemplated my career to this point, I started to ask myself a lot of questions.

- What happened?
- Where did I go wrong?
- What do others think about me?
- Is this it? Is this what I'm supposed to do for the rest of my life?

Have you ever asked yourself any of these questions before?

For weeks afterward I struggled to find answers to these questions. And for weeks I continued to come up empty on my own, so I turned to Google. I Googled career crisis and midlife crisis. I read all the resources I could find. I found nothing helpful. It seemed there was no solution for my problem.

Then one day during my commute, I was listening to a podcast when a glimmer of hope hit me.

The show featured an interview with an executive career coach. The topic was personal branding. I'd never heard of personal branding before, but I do remember when I heard it, I knew immediately this was a big part of my problem. I couldn't explain it, but I knew I needed to develop my personal brand.

Two days later I hired the coach from the podcast. Over the course of next three months, she walked me through the steps of defining my personal brand. This was the beginning of my career transformation.

Wait? I'm Not the Only One?

One of the first things I learned about personal branding is that it is a process. Unfortunately, as personal branding expert Jane Anderson told me during our interview, many people want to skirt the process and not put in the work required to build their brand the right way.

Instead, Jane told me, they approach personal branding as if it's "something you would buy if you have too much money. 'I'd like a personal brand, please. Here's my credit card.'"

Your personal brand is not something you can order and have shipped to you—not by a long shot. Your personal brand is a something you develop over time. What my coach helped me realize during our time together is the importance of understanding and building your brand for your career.

This realization finally hit me on a Saturday afternoon as I was completing an assigned exercise. The exercise was to take an honest look at what I wanted my life to look like in three to five years.

As I was thinking through where I wanted to be in the future, I considered my ideal job, my ideal workplace, my ideal customers (more on this later), and the different technologies that were in place then and how they could be used to help build my brand.

Being a natural thinker (something I discovered as I went through this process), I started to wonder how I could use my LinkedIn profile to complement my resume and how I could use both to enhance my brand.

Then another thought occurred to me. How do I show up in a Google search?

While not part of the exercise, I decided to find out. So for the first time ever, I typed my name, Ryan Rhoten, into the search bar and hit enter. The results completely surprised me. I realized instantly that I had a problem.

On the surface, you would think my name is pretty unique. I expected to see me on the first page of results. Instead, I discovered I'm not the only Ryan Rhoten in the world. There are four of us.

I didn't show up in the search results until page four, and I was result number eight or nine on that page, nearly 40 results after the first one. I remember thinking to myself, *Nobody is ever going to find me online.* I mean, who looks past page one?

As bad as this sounds—and it is bad for your career, as you'll learn through the course of this book—what was on page one was even worse. One of the other Ryans dominated page one with four or five of the top ten search results.

Why? Because he had recently been arrested, again, for selling drugs.

As soon as I saw this, it hit me hard. This is what people were finding when they searched for me online. They didn't discover the years of industry experience I have, nor did they see the accomplishments and awards I'd earned over the years. Heck, my LinkedIn profile didn't even show up!

Instead, I was nonexistent, invisible, while the recently arrested person who shares my name was anything but invisible. People searching for me were finding him. Recruiters, hiring managers, potential business clients—they would all find him and not me.

The Game Has Changed

"Be the change you wish to see in the world."
—Mahatma Gandhi

During my personal brand journey, a friend recommended a book written by Donald Miller called *A Million Miles in a Thousand Years*. The author applies the plot points of a narrative story to our personal lives. One of the plot points he described still stands out in my mind. That plot point is called an inciting incident.

An inciting incident is a place in the story where a problem begins and the protagonist—you in this case—must decide on a path, like Neo from the Matrix choosing the red pill over the blue one.

We all experience inciting incidents in our lives, and if we look at our lives as a narrative, I think you'd agree we are all living out a story. In this story, everything leading up our inciting incidents is considered the backstory. The backstory provides context for what is to come. Our careers are no exception.

Our career backstory consists of our jobs, our promotions, our experiences, our skills, and our traits. All work together to feed our backstory and provide us with a path along our perceived futures. As you progress along your career narrative, you will also experience inciting incidents.

Some will be of your choosing, while others will come as a complete surprise to you. Whatever your inciting incident is, one thing remains true for each and every one of us. Once we reach it, we have a decision to make. Again, red pill or blue pill?

At this point in the book, I've already provided you with my backstory as well as two inciting incidents. The first inciting incident, my non-promotion, made me consider my path and where my career was headed. I choose the red pill and discovered personal branding.

My second inciting incident was the realization that I was invisible online. This made me consider my online presence and what my friends and my company would think about me. Again I choose the red pill, and this time I discovered the importance of managing one's online reputation.

My inciting incidents left me with simple choices, as yours will do. You can choose the blue pill and carry on with your life and your career. Or you can choose the red pill and discover what you were ultimately meant to become.

Too many people choose to take the blue pill. Maybe they're afraid to rock the boat. Maybe they're afraid to "put themselves out there." The reality is that they've grown comfortable with their life and position. There's nothing wrong with this path. I was on it for most of my life. I was complacent as well.

It took my inciting incidents to open my eyes and recognize that I was the one holding myself back. Not the boss who didn't promote me, and not Google for putting me on page four. It was me.

If my career was going to change, I had to change. I had to adapt to a new way of looking at my career. It was no longer a straight path or a ladder. No one was watching over my shoulder and telling me what to do next. I needed to own my career because no one else was going to own it for me.

It's been nearly five years now since I took that first metaphorical red pill. During this time, I've asked myself a lot of questions I never imagined before. The questions were always there; I just couldn't see them.

This book is my attempt to help you begin to ask and answer those questions for yourself so you can "plan" your inciting incident rather than have it find you one Friday afternoon. Whatever career formula you have been following, I promise you it has changed. This book will help you discover a new formula.

Looking back, I now know that if I had worked on building my brand sooner, I may never have written this book because I would have received that promotion. Instead, I didn't get the promotion and as a result you're holding five years worth of research from books, blog posts, and seventy-five interviews with career coaches, recruiters, hiring managers, and personal brand experts.

That's the power of the red pill, but as Morpheus tells Neo, you have to see it for yourself. So if you're ready, remember, all I'm offering is the truth about how to build your brand in a way that will get you recognized by raising your visibility online.

This is the new formula for career success and satisfaction today. The good news is that you can define what success looks like for you. This book will help you get there by leveraging tools already available to you, if you're willing to step out of your comfort zone.

Chapter 2

About This Book

This book started out as a research project for myself, after being turned down for a promotion and discovering that I am not the only Ryan Rhoten in the world.

In it, you will find everything I know about personal brands, digital brands, and the importance of both for your career. I'll also introduce to you a new word I've coined that I believe sums up perfectly what it takes to stand out and distinguish yourself from others in your field today.

The game has changed. You need to change with it. This book will show you how.

Additionally, I'll introduce you to the Digital Brand Assessment and the DICE process. The assessment is designed to get you started, and the DICE process will you help build and establish your digital brand in order to help you get recognized for your expertise.

What This Book Is Not

Before we dive into the content, I think it's important you understand what this book is NOT.

This is NOT a how-to job search book. Although the methodology outlined in the book will certainly help you as a job seeker attract new and exciting opportunities, this is not the purpose of this book.

This book is NOT a how-to resume book. If you need help with your resume, do not buy this book. It will not help you. If you are looking for job search and resume help, here are six books I recommend you read:

The Career Upgrade Roadmap: 90 Days to a Better Job and a Better Life by Olivia Gamber
Repurpose Your Career: A Practical Guide for Baby Boomers by Marc Miller
60 Seconds and You're Hired! by Robin Ryan
Navigating Career Crossroads: How to Thrive When Changing Direction by Jane Jackson
The Resume Coloring Book by Lea McLeod
Impact: How to Build your Personal Brand in the Connection Economy by Jane Anderson

I have personally read all of these books as well as interviewed the authors. They are excellent guides on how to conduct a job search and update your resume in today's career environment.

You can listen to my interviews with each of the authors on my podcast, *The BRAND New You Show*. I discuss each author's book and methodology in detail. So much detail, in fact, that listening to them as you read through the book will help to solidify the concepts in your mind.

This book is NOT a "quick win" book. Completing the exercises in this book will take you some time, especially during the first step in DICE as you work to define your brand. Building your brand requires you to ask questions you've never asked before, such as:

- What do others (your boss, your peers, your friends) really think about you?
- What do they say about you when you're not in the room?

Knowing how others perceive you is immensely powerful because once you know, you can begin to change your behavior if needed. Referencing the old adage of "don't fix what ain't broke," how do you know something "ain't broke" if you don't ask the right questions? The answer to these questions is the difference between getting promoted or not. If you're not willing to ask and answer these questions, this book will not help you, as the answers you discover are the foundation for the rest of the book.

Chapter 3

The Digital Brand Assessment

I launched the Digital Brand Assessment in January 2015. Its purpose is to help you understand your digital brand. Like it or not, you have one, but the key is how you manage it—which unfortunately many don't.

We live in a digital-first world, meaning that your online presence (i.e., your digital brand) speaks for you long before you have a chance to speak for yourself. This will only grow more prevalent as time moves on. Because of this, I believe the best opportunities in the future—and the future is now, by the way—will go to those who take the time to define what they want to be known for and then reinforce that in everything they do, both online and offline.

If you are afraid to put yourself out there, if you believe you don't need an online presence, or if you feel your experiences and skills should speak for themselves, you will be left behind. In the words of the soup Nazi from Seinfeld, there will be "no opportunities for you."

Each year in December, I update the assessment and relaunch it in January. The updates, like iterations in software development, consist of adding any new things I've learned throughout the year as well as fixing any "bugs" I've discovered along the way. Bugs are any confusing questions, feedback, or comments I've received from individuals who have taken the assessment.

By far, the most common piece of feedback I've received comes in the form of a question. "How do I get started building my digital brand?" This book is the answer to that question.

Since its initial launch, over three thousand people have taken the assessment and received their digital brand score—a rating between zero and 100. A score of 100 indicates that you have a perfect digital brand. Some have come close, but none have met it. The average score at the time of this writing is 30, which isn't bad, but it's not enough to get you noticed or send opportunities your way. If you haven't taken the assessment yet, I encourage you to do so at this point.

Exercise 1—Take the Digital Brand Assessment

This first exercise is simple: Take a few minutes to complete the digital brand assessment. The questions as well as your resulting score will help you as you dive into the content within this book. You can find the assessment at http://ryanrhoten.com.

To get an accurate result, you need to do a couple of things before you take the assessment. The instructions provided are for using the Google Chrome browser.

1. Log out of browser—SELECT YOUR NAME TOP RIGHT > SWITCH PERSON
2. Clear browser cache—SETTINGS > HISTORY > CLEAR BROWSING DATA
3. Open a private browser—FILE > NEW INCOGNITO WINDOW

All browsers store information about your searches online. Staying logged into your browser will not give you the same results as someone else who may be searching for you, such as a recruiter, hiring manager, or even me.

Logging out of your browser and clearing your cache allows you to get a more accurate picture of how you appear online. Once your browser is set, you'll be able to take the assessment in exchange for an email address by clicking the orange button.

Upon completion you will be presented with your digital brand score. You will also find a link directly below your score that will take you to a page explaining what the score means and the steps you can take to start improving your digital brand.

Chapter 4

How to Use This Book

This book walks you through a step-by-step process designed to take you from confusion about your personal and digital brand to a "now I get it" mindset—but only if you follow the steps.

The book is divided into seven parts revolving around two key aspects: your digital brand assessment score and the DICE process. Part One introduces you to the main aspects of the book. In Part Two: CareerKred, we'll discuss the increased importance of standing out in your career and how you can leverage your digital brand to boost your CareerKred.

We will begin diving into the DICE process in Part Three: The Define Step. This step will help you discover your brand. In Part Four: The Integrate Step, you'll learn the importance of integrating your brand digitally and how to do so strategically and on purpose. Part Five: The Create Step, may be a challenge for you as you learn how to create content relevant to your brand. Part Six: The Engage Step concludes the deep dive into the DICE process. Here you will learn how to leverage your online brand and content and discover a few social media tools to really expand your reach.

Part Seven, simply called The Wrap, will bring together everything discussed throughout the book and hopefully push you toward the red pill.

You've heard the expression, "It's simple but not easy", right? The DICE process is a real life example of this spelled out between the covers of this book. Some exercises will be simple, and easy others will be simple and hard. They will *all* push you out of your comfort zone.

Exercises

To get the most from this book, you'll need to complete the exercises. Yes, you will learn things you can apply simply by reading, but completing the exercises will ensure that you have a complete personal and digital brand when you're finished.

To help you complete the exercises and keep all of your discoveries in one place, I have created a companion workbook for this book. You can download a copy of this workbook at http://CareerKredBook.com/workbook.

I think you'll find this a useful resource not just while reading the book but over time as well because your personal brand can and will change.

The Digital Brand Assessment and DICE

The digital brand assessment and the DICE process are interwoven; they both feed each other. Each section of the DICE process outlined in this book will start with the correlating assessment score, as well as a description of what the score could mean for you.

This is not to say you should start reading the book in the section correlated to your assessment score. Remember, the point is to walk through the DICE process step-by-step. That said, I understand your need to get to the solution that works best for you. Here is how the digital brand assessment aligns with the DICE process.

1. Define your brand: 0—25 (35)
2. Integrate your brand online (your digital brand): 26—50
3. Create content for your brand: 51—75
4. Engage with your audience: 76—100

Let me reiterate. This process works best if followed step-by-step from the beginning. My hope, as you progress through each step, is that you'll understand and see the benefit of following the process. Some of you will think, *I already know my brand, so I'm moving right to step two.* Others may be eager to start creating content.

Here's the funny thing, though: Building your brand is a never-ending process. Every day I learn things about branding that surprise me. That's why I update the assessment every year. Your brand, even if you feel you know it well, will still benefit by taking another peek at it.

The DICE process is not a straight-line process where you go from point A to point B and finish. Rather, it's a circular process that starts over and repeats itself once you've completed the exercises in the last step.

Chapter 5

Why This Book Is Important

You might be asking yourself, "Why is all this branding stuff so important?" I believe the answer has both macro and micro components—macro being the intangible things that impact us, such as the changing career landscape, new technologies, and so on. Micro components, on the other hand, cause us to change our position or behaviors whether we want to or not. It's the Alan Deutschman philosophy of "change or die."

The micro components are influenced by the macro ones. They are more personal in nature, and they usually have a choice associated with them. I referred to these components earlier as inciting incidents. You can also call them warning shots across the bow. They should make you stand up and take notice.

Since the great recession, there have been tremendous changes, both macro and micro, in the career landscape. Let's start with the macro components. Thanks to technology we are seeing continuous changes in the way we work and where we work. This is will only accelerate in the coming years.

This acceleration is causing us to reevaluate the world of work we have come to know and accept. This ain't our parents career workplace anymore. Opportunities don't fall to those who can weather out the storm of retirements and the upward promotions that usually accompany them. Those opportunities are few and far between as more and more baby boomers are staying employed longer.

"You Must Kill Your Darlings"

Little did William Faulkner know that his phrase "In writing, you must kill all your darlings" could be applied in so many scenarios. The career space is filled with old methods and processes that many still cling to.

In the context of this book, "killing your darlings" means forgetting everything you've been taught about traditional career paths so you can chart a new course.

According to the Future of Work Study conducted by Price Water House Coopers,[1] by the year 2020 40 percent of the workforce in the United States will be freelancers. 2020 is not far away—will you be ready for it?

If you doubt this, take a look around. Have you seen any of your peers laid off in recent years? Have you been laid off? Have you seen jobs you thought were steady positions within a company become obsolete seemingly overnight because of the introduction of a new technology? I think we all have.

This is why you need to prepare now for what author Taylor Pearson refers to as "the end of jobs." During our discussion about his book by the same name, Taylor mentioned a startling statistic: Since 2000 the world's population has outpaced jobs by 2.4 percent. This means the world produces more people than there are jobs available for them.

There are a multitude of reasons for this, and chief among them is every corporation's desire to increase its efficiencies and reduce its costs. You and I, my friends, are costs. In the past, companies could reduce costs by shifting manufacturing locations, introducing new technology in the manufacturing process, or a combination of both.

These changes typically only impacted blue-collar positions.

This has led a lot of white collar folks to believe that their jobs are safe. This is a dangerous mindset and one that Taylor and I discussed at length during the podcast when he introduced me to a concept known as "silent risk."

He summarized silent risk perfectly by telling the following story of Tom the Turkey and comparing Tom to a real life friend he referred to as Max the Accountant.

Tom the Turkey

All of us began accumulating silent risk the day we started our careers, not unlike a turkey on a farm. From the moment a turkey

1 Rendell, M. & Brown, J. (2105). *The Future of Work: A Journey to 2022*, 23. Retrieved from http://www.pwc.com/gx/en/issues/talent/future-of-work/journey-to-2022.html.

is born, it is looked after and fed. Every day the turkey wakes up and uses the previous days to determine what the current day will look like.

Because Tom the Turkey is looking backward to determine its present and future, every day looks bright and normal. Tom is confident he will be fed and allowed to do his job—whatever the job of a turkey is on a daily basis.

Life goes on this way for Tom the Turkey until Thanksgiving Day when the farmer shows up with an axe.

Does this example seem far-fetched? If so, let me ask you a question. Have you or your peers ever been given notice that the farmer was coming prior to the day he or she showed up? Of course not. In the cases I've personally witnessed, peers who were let go had no idea it was coming. The farmer just showed up with the axe.

Max the Accountant is no different than Tom the Turkey. Max started building up silent risk the day he began working. Every day, he came to work, did his job, and did it well, only to go home at the end of the day and start the cycle again in the morning.

Nothing in Max's past would have led him to believe that this life he had created for himself through his hard work would ever go away. Max prepared for his future by earning advanced degrees in business and tax law.

Unfortunately, like many people, Max was using his past to predict his future. As a result, he didn't notice that people on the other side of the world—the Philippines, for example—were also going to college and earning accounting and other advanced degrees. Some even specialized in tax law.

As Max was working hard at his job, his employers were looking for efficiencies and cost reductions. As they searched, they discovered overseas accounting businesses who specialized in accounting and tax laws but at half the cost of their current accounting department budget.

Max the Accountant had no idea until the farmer showed up at his office.

The Democratization of Credentials

Many of you will argue with me on this point, but an advanced degree such as an MBA doesn't mean the same thing it used to. If you doubt me, think about this. If you had two candidates you were considering for a position, one who had recently graduated with an MBA, and the other who didn't have an MBA but had a wealth of experience that could be applied now, who would you hire?

For me personally, I will always hire for experience over a degree.

Degrees today don't mean what they once did. Degrees, especially advanced degrees, used to be rare. If you had one, you were worth more in the marketplace. The introduction of the Internet has changed this—I think for the better.

Credentials in the form of degrees, certificates, or certifications are a dime a dozen today. It seems everyone has one. The Internet has made this possible. Colleges now put the entire curriculum for some degrees online for free. If you have the discipline and time, you can earn a college degree at a fraction of the cost and from the comfort of your home.

It is easy to relate credentials to the law of supply and demand. When credentials or advanced degrees were in short supply, the demand for them resulted in higher compensation for the few who had them. However, we have now reached a point where credentials and advanced degrees are no longer in short supply. In some fields, we may even be at a saturation point. Think back to the story of Max the Accountant. Max was competing against people all over the globe with the same degree.

This overabundance of credentials is causing the job market to reassess their worth. Today, credential holders no longer command the higher compensation that once accompanied their degree. Instead, these degrees have become the starting point for a job description.

Don't take this section the wrong way; I'm not advocating against advanced degrees. But because credentials are more easily obtained today and will only become more accessible to the world as a whole in the future, credentials aren't viewed the same way they have been in the past.

In the future, what will separate you from your competition is your brand, along with your demonstrable experience.

Taylor and others like him believe that "your track record is the new credential." Your experiences and expertise—i.e., your brand—might be what gets you a particular position that once would have required a degree to obtain.

Let's Get Personal

Besides the higher-level macro reasons this book is important, there are also some micro, personal reasons it's worth your time to read. I could start with the obvious and suggest it's because you yourself have been turned down for a promotion—a promotion you felt you deserved.

If this describes you, I am truly sorry. I feel your pain.

Outside of not getting a promotion, perhaps you feel stuck or bored in your career. This happens, especially since many of us are urged to choose a career path at a young age with no real concept of what a career really means. Perhaps you were just following the process your parents taught you.

Boredom in your career has a funny way of getting compounded with the responsibilities of life. You have bills to pay, a mortgage or rent, maybe children to feed, and of course saving for college, which effectively starts the cycle over again for your children.

All this "stuff" causes you to stay in a job or a career not because you want to but because you feel you have to. When this happens you lose some of your zeal for your work. It becomes routine. You roll into your office, you put in your hours, and if you're lucky you get moved around into different departments. This helps for a little while, but it doesn't help you shake the feeling that you're stuck.

You want more, but you're not exactly sure what. You are not alone. Here are some other micro reasons that may resonate with you.

- You are not really aware of "your brand."
- You don't know what your brand is supposed to be.
- You struggle to identify where you add the most value.
- You can't figure out your "why and what you want to say about yourself."
- You are searching for your field of expertise or your niche.
- You want to discover your strengths.

All of these are very personal, micro level reasons for reading this book. We'll address them all—how you can identify your brand, what your strengths are, what to say about yourself, and even how to find your field of expertise.

This book will also cover things such as how to build your online presence the right way so you can get noticed by recruiters, hiring managers, and people you don't yet know who can help your career.

This book will show you the right way to use the tools at your disposal, such as websites and social media, to increase your visibility and build your digital brand. We'll even cover ways you can position yourself as a subject matter expert while balancing corporate and personal branding.

Everything covered in this book is real and has been applied to myself and my clients. But for any of it to work, there is one key tenet you must adhere to, and that is the notion that you are indeed a brand.

Management guru Tom Peters said it best in his article for *Fast Company* magazine in 1997:

> "It's this simple: You are a brand. You are in charge of your brand. There is no single path to success. And there is no one right way to create the brand called You. Except this: Start today. Or else."[2]

So if you're ready to take charge of your brand and push the career mindset of Tom the Turkey to the side, let's get started.

---

2 Peters, T. (1997). *The Brand Called You.* Retrieved from https://www.fastcompany.com/28905/brand-called-you.

Part Two

CareerKred

"Every action or perceived inaction shapes credibility."
—Mindy Hall

Chapter 6

Is Your Brand Costing You Opportunities?

"Our lives are defined by opportunities, even the ones we miss."—F. Scott Fitzgerald

Repeat after me: "I am a brand."

Try it again. This time say it out loud. Acknowledging that you are a brand will change the way you look at your career. I know it changed the way I look at mine.

Say it again. "I am a brand."

If that sentence scares you or makes you shake you head in disbelief, maybe this book is not for you. If, on the other hand, you believe you are a brand or think you may be one, keep reading.

Even after my coach and I finished our time together, it still took awhile for this concept to sink in because, up until that point, I had always thought brands were for big companies. You probably feel the same way.

Generally speaking, a brand is a name, term, design, symbol, or other feature that distinguishes one seller's product from those of other sellers. The same is true if you apply this to your career. Like a brand, you and I have features such as skills, traits, and expertise that distinguish us from others.

If you are not quite ready to acknowledge you are brand just yet, then let's at least agree for now that from a career standpoint, you are different from others, even if you do the exact same job as someone else.

This notion is critical to the mindset you need in order to grasp and apply the concepts in this book. Whether you see it yet or not, you are a brand in the eyes of others, and for this book to make sense to you, you must also see this in yourself.

To help you grasp this notion, what if you and I were speaking at a conference and I mentioned coffee? What is the first thing that comes to your mind?

Chances are two things happened. First, you probably thought of a brand like Starbucks or Dunkin Donuts. Second, you may have felt some type of emotion when you thought about the brand.

The emotion you experienced could be good or bad. Whichever it is, it was formed by your perception and/or experience with the brand. That's why you perceive some brands as great and others as not so good. Your emotions may have been formed as the result of very good customer service or perhaps the opposite.

Either way, when you hear a particular brand mentioned out loud, your emotions come to the surface and you have a very distinct reaction/opinion about the brand.

If you doubt this, I challenge you to ask twenty random people what they think about Starbucks. Do you think all twenty will give you the exact same answer? No, because brand perception is different for everyone.

Personal brands are no different.

If we were talking at the same conference and instead of coffee I said the word product manager, who is the first person that comes to your mind? If you don't know any product managers, then pretend I said tax accountant, attorney, business analyst, or marketing manager? If none of those titles work for you, feel free to substitute your own.

My point here is that whoever's name came to your mind when you thought about the job title I mentioned, that person has differentiated themselves from their competition. Their brand stands out in your mind. Maybe you had a great experience with them on a project or you've seen the work they do from afar. Either way, a person's brand elicits the same emotions as a business brand in your mind and the minds of others.

Still struggling with the concept that you are a brand? This might help. According to Jerry McLaughlin's article on Forbes.com[(3)], a brand is:

> [A brand is] what your peers think of when he or she hears your name. It's everything the public thinks it knows about your name

brand offering—both factual, and emotional. Your brand name exists objectively; people can see it. It's fixed.[3]

In other words, your brand is ultimately the perception others have about you. It's how they distinguish you from someone else.

In the context of your career, your brand is held by anyone you've ever interacted with, from your peers to your bosses. Every day at work, you reinforce and build your brand. If you've built a good brand in other's eyes, it's possible for opportunities to come your way.

On the other hand, if you haven't focused on building your brand and instead left it to chance like Max the Accountant, opportunities will most likely go to someone else.

"Ryan, you didn't get the position."

The Old-School Process

"You must unlearn what you have learned." —Yoda

It was neither by accident or intention that I arrived at my career crisis. It was mostly ignorance—ignorance from not understanding I was a brand, from not taking the time to develop my brand, and ignorance from not recognizing the value in distinguishing myself from my competition.

Personal branding expert and author of the books *Reinventing You* and *Stand Out* Dorie Clark told me during our interview, "Standing out (in your career) is no longer an option. It's a necessity." I get this now. I didn't then.

At the time, I thought you stood out in your career by working hard and putting in the time. This was the process my parents followed, and it seemed to work for them. Perhaps you've heard this before.

Get good grades. Go to college. Get a good job. Work Hard. Live happily ever after.—Mom

---

3 McLaughlin, J. (2011). *What is a Brand, Anyway?* Retrieved from http://www.forbes.com/sites/jerrymclaughlin/2011/12/21/what-is-a-brand-anyway/#57355f572aa4.

Do you subscribe to this philosophy today? I followed this process for most of my career. In fact, I followed it right up to the point of hearing the words, "You didn't get the position." The process that worked so well for our parents no longer works today.

Like many of you, when I got out of college, I followed my parents' formula. I worked hard, and initially my hard work was rewarded with promotions. In hindsight, the promotions only served to strengthen my belief in the process because for the first few years of my career, I was promoted on average once every nine months.

Like an obedient child, I followed the process to a "T," and I was happy. I was moving up the corporate ladder just like my parents encouraged me to do. I was distinguishing myself from my peers and earning credibility. I was also building up silent risk because the process worked like a charm. Until, one day, it didn't.

You know about that day for me, but what about you? Have you experienced a time when the formula handed down from your parents stopped working? If you have, on that day you started to question everything.

What was it for you? Was it a promotion you didn't? Or was it the day you got your annual review and discovered your boss didn't think you had done as good a job as the previous year? Maybe it was the day you realized your competition for an open position lived on the other side of the world. Whatever it was, it had the same effect on you.

All of a sudden, you felt stuck on whichever rung of the corporate ladder you happened to find yourself. Here's a little secret. There never really was a corporate ladder. It's something somebody, maybe our parents, made up in order to comfort us and keep us moving forward when the days were rough. The problem is, the same "comfort" the ladder provided during those rough days also lulls us to sleep.

Not actual sleep, mind you (unless your name is George Costanza), but the kind of sleep that causes you to become comfortable. The kind of sleep where looking backward convinces you the future is bright. The kind of sleep that drives you to complacency.

And complacency is a career killer.

The simple truth is that you can't stand out when you are complacent. When you reach this point, there is no chance you will be differentiated from your peers. Your skills, traits and expertise will become hidden in an alphabet soup of corporate titles and jargon—and worse, you might start to like it that way.

You might begin to believe that if you hang on long enough, you'll get the promotion and the salary you deserve. After all, you've got an MBA and all those certifications to boot. But here is something you might have forgotten as you advanced in your career.

You get what you earn.

Complacency causes you to turn this truth around in your head and makes you believe you have already earned what you want.

This mindset is dangerous to your brand. It's a slippery slope that's hard to overcome—just ask Max the Accountant. In fact, if you don't recognize the symptoms, you may never move past it. The brand that once got you recognized as a leader and provided you with new challenges and promotions will begin to fade in the minds of others.

When this happens, you'll find yourself no longer being called upon to take on new projects. You'll watch from the sidelines as others get promoted around you. Your well-respected and hard-earned brand has "suddenly" become less respected, and your credibility begins to dim with it.

Slowly you recognize this is happening and you look for a way to change things, but unfortunately for you, you only know one way, one path, one process for career success: the old-school process that hasn't kept up with the changing times.

If you've read this far, then I believe you are ready to learn a new process, a process that will unfold throughout this book. This new process works in the social world we find ourselves living in, but there is a catch.

The process relies on YOU, not a corporation, for your career success.

As I said earlier, it all starts with you viewing yourself as a business, a brand—or, as my friend and host of *The Voice of Job Seekers* podcast Mark Anthony Dyson says, a consultant—not as an employee. Because as you will discover throughout this book, you are way more than an employee. You are, in fact, a brand.

Chapter 7

Workplace Credibility

After all of my research and interviews with personal branding and career experts, I've come to believe that the key to career satisfaction, advancement, and maybe even happiness is credibility. If you have it, you can go far. If you don't, well, "Ryan, you're not getting the position."

Credibility is the key to career success. If you doubt this, answer the following questions.

Would you attend a training course run by someone with no experience in the subject?
Would you buy from a salesperson who doesn't know anything about her product or service?
Would you go "above and beyond" for a leader who didn't keep his word?
Would you hire someone for a position who didn't demonstrate that he or she could perform in the role?

If you are like me, you'd answer "no" to all of these questions. Why? Because if you're going to invest your time, energy, and enthusiasm in someone, you want that person to be credible—i.e., worthy of your trust.

Credibility comes from the root word *credo*, which in Latin means "I believe." Taking a slightly more modern look at the word *credibility* we find that, according to the *Urban Dictionary*, credibility is *"the quality of being believable or trustworthy."*

A quick Google search for credibility returns this definition: "The quality of being trusted and believed in and the quality of being convincing or believable."

Put simply, credibility is the trust others assign you because of your experiences or actions. Your credibility can help influence people's behaviors as well as their thoughts about you or your area of expertise.

If you, as someone who is seeking a promotion or a new job, are not credible, hiring managers and recruiters will be less likely to trust you. Being credible is what helps people believe that you are worthy of the job at hand.

Credibility portrays you as trustworthy and believable in whatever task you do. Whether you are giving a presentation, delivering training, or selling your ideas, it's credibility that pushes you forward.

Building Your Credibility

If credibility is so important, how can you build it? Unfortunately, there is no single thing that creates credibility. Rather, credibility comes from a combination of things that must be in place in order for you to earn it.

Old-school credibility, like the kind our parents earned, included things like hours worked, projects completed, and maybe even one's arrival time at work. Today credibility encompasses all this plus so much more.

I believe credibility is a by-product of building your brand; it takes time, patience, and consistency.

Credibility also requires character, and building your character requires an understanding of yourself at a deeper level than you do today. For one thing, you need to know your core values. Understanding your values allows you to stand up for what you believe in. This is especially true if your stance is contrary to popular opinion.

More than anything, credibility requires you to become self-aware. You need to know your strengths, what you enjoy, what you are currently known for, and what you want to be known for in the future.

It's hard to build trust and have others believe in you when you don't have an awareness of these things.

Define Your Expertise

"99 percent of my clients know what they don't want, but they don't know what they do want." —Jane Anderson

Credibility comes from focusing your self-awareness, meaning you need to be known for something. Without being known for something in your career, it is difficult to establish yourself as an expert.

Jane Anderson, personal brand expert and author of the book *Impact*, explained it this way: "You need to become known for knowing something as opposed to knowing something."

Take a minute and reread Jane's comment. The distinction is subtle but important. We all know something—something about our jobs, our hobbies, or our passions. But do others also know us for that knowledge?

The way to become known for knowing something is by doing something. When you can demonstrate your expertise in a subject matter, whether through experiences or the content you create, you become credible in other people's eyes. But you can't become known for knowing something if you haven't taken the time to define what you want to be known for in the first place.

Think back to the opening question in this section. Would you attend a training course put on by someone who has no experience in the subject? Of course you wouldn't. Because in your mind and everyone else's for that matter, they have no credibility on the subject.

Like your brand, you build your expertise and your credibility each and every day. It can usually be found in a single area or skill set that is unique to you. Your expertise can be in an area within your company or outside of it.

Chances are you don't recognize it now, but you will after you've completed the Define step.

Establish Your Expertise

People who have expertise just love to share it.
—David Baldacci

If you and I were to meet at a bar for drinks, and I asked you what you were an expert at, what would your answer be? You either know an answer right away or you don't. A lot my clients can answer this question right away. Many of them truly know what they want to be known for. Some want to be known as an expert in accounting, others in engineering, model airplanes, the latest technology, or even podcasting.

Whichever it is for you, the "what" matters much less than the "who"—as in who knows you're an expert besides yourself?

Today an important part of being credible and trustworthy in other people's eyes is establishing your expertise online. You see, "expert" is a title you can give yourself, but it's much more powerful when others bestow it on you.

Being called an expert by someone else makes you instantly credible to other people. Once you earn this moniker, it's important to protect and reinforce it in whatever area you are known for. The best way to be credible and demonstrate your expertise today is to be found in a Google search.

This is the beginning of being known for knowing something.

During the Integrate step, we will walk through how to integrate your brand online so you show up in search engines in a way that emphasizes your expertise and showcases whatever it is you want to be known for so that others can recognize it.

Would you attend a training course run by someone who shows up on the first page of Google? Of course you would. Todd Lohenry, a Search Engine Optimization (SEO) expert, told me during our podcast interview:

> Showing up in search automatically imparts a certain level of authority and credibility to you. If there are two candidates for a job opening, the person who demonstrates they have done the work is the person who has a leg up in the process, all other things being equal.

To put this in context, as a hiring manager, would you place preference on a candidate who shows up in search demonstrating expertise in the area for which you are looking to hire over a candidate who only provides a resume?

I'm guessing you would, and that's the power of integrating your expertise into your brand online. It helps you demonstrate your work while also adding credibility to your name.

Communication Creates Credibility

"Communication—the human connection—is the key to personal and career success." —Paul J. Meyer

Just as in the offline world, your communication skills in the online world play an important role in your credibility. Communication is the way people get to know and like you. However, in order for you to communicate your expertise or your message, you need a platform from which to do it. This is why I believe a website is so important today in establishing your credibility online.

If you don't have a platform, my friend Shane Purnell, host of the *Platform Giant* podcast, will tell you: You may need to CARVE one out for yourself.

You CARVE your platform through communication, both online and offline. In order for people to see you as credible, you not only need to show up in search engines, but you need to show up for whatever it is you want to be known for. One of the best ways to do this is to voice your thoughts and opinions to the world through a blog.

You'll also want to communicate your thoughts through social media and other online platforms. To become known for what you know, you must take a stance and create content that is unique to you and your expertise. Doing so allows people to understand the depth of your knowledge and form an opinion of you.

This is a key part of becoming credible in someone's eyes. If you consistently demonstrate your knowledge and thoughts about your area of expertise, people will begin to see you as the expert.

Would you hire a person you didn't believe in?

Build Your Tribe

As you begin to establish credibility, a funny thing happens. People start to seek you out. They ask you for your advice, your opinion, your thoughts in your area of expertise. You will also begin to attract like-minded people.

When this happens, you must be able to engage with them.

It can take a long time to build up your credibility, but only a conversation to destroy it. Think back to the definition of credibility: "The quality of being believable or trustworthy." If someone were to ask you to have a conversation, and you said yes but then ignored them, do you think this would impact your credibility in that person's eyes?

If you were a hiring manager, would you hire a candidate that appears highly qualified, has the expertise you are looking for, but won't return your calls? Of course you wouldn't, and neither would I.

In the Engage step, we'll discuss all the different ways you can maintain and boost your credibility.

Influence

A side effect of building your brand and credibility is influence. *Influence*, according to the Urban Dictionary, is "the power to change, encourage, or make a difference without force."

Influence is also "the capacity to have an effect on the character, development, or behavior of someone or something."

In other words, influence means you are able to affect action. As a career professional, your goal is to influence hiring managers and recruiters to make the right decision—i.e., hire you.

The more you demonstrate your expertise, the more credibility, influence, and authority you will have in other people's minds. The authority they impart to you in their minds only comes after you've established a certain level of "I know what I am talking about." Or as Marc Miller, career coach and host of the *Repurpose Your Career* podcast, likes to say, "You've answered the question, 'How do I know that you know your stuff?'"

Chapter 8

CareerKred

"If people like you they will listen to you, but if they trust you, they'll do business with you." —Zig Ziglar

Credibility plays a huge role in your career. However, chances are good you don't recognize it in yourself. Credibility is what gets you promoted, it's what sends opportunities your way and not someone else's way. When you get opportunities that others do not, it's because people see you as not just capable but also credible. You are both believable and trustworthy in their eyes.

As I mentioned earlier, you build credibility and demonstrate capability each and every day throughout your career. With each successful project you complete, experience you gain, or blog post you write, you are earning trust and building influence. You are becoming more and more credible.

I'll take a leap here and assume that everyone who reads this book has heard of the term *street cred*. The Urban Dictionary defines *street cred* as "commanding a level of respect in an urban environment due to experience in or knowledge of issues affecting those environments."

While your experiences in an urban environment may be minimal, you can earn "street cred" in the corporate environment due to your experience and knowledge in your area of expertise. I call this CareerKred.

CareerKred is the influence and trust you earn through your actions and experiences as they relate to your career.

A quick note here about the word *career*. A career is defined as a profession that someone does for a long time. A profession on the other hand is a job that requires special education, training, or skills, while a job is simply the work that a person does regularly in order to earn money.

For the purpose of this book, a career is the work you do to earn money on a regular basis that requires education, training, and skills. This includes work in a corporate environment, a start-up, freelancing, coaching, or even work you do from home on the side. CareerKred is not tied to a specific type of job.

Like street cred, CareerKred is earned over time. It provides the social proof you need to show you can indeed change, encourage, and make a difference in the lives of individuals and businesses you work with.

When you have CareerKred, people recognize it and are drawn to you. They trust what you say and believe you are the right person for the job. Your CareerKred is what will drive opportunities to you.

CareerKred Used to Be Local

Like the Force in *Star Wars*, CareerKred has always been with you. It started the moment you took your first job, and you've been building it or losing it ever since.

There's something interesting about CareerKred, though. Not long ago, it was only earned locally. The only people who acknowledged your CareerKred were the people in your building, your office, or your company. The exception to this was if you worked directly with clients and customers.

Unless you had an insider connection to another company, your CareerKred was largely non-existent to anyone outside of your company. That's how the resume became so important in the job search process. How would a company know about your CareerKred if you didn't provide it to them? The resume served this purpose.

Within your company, your CareerKred was earned your through your actions and interactions with others. You came to work, did a great job, and people took notice. Hopefully your CareerKred was recognized by those "above" you and you were rewarded either with a promotion—or if you weren't quite ready for a promotion, you might have been placed in a company-sponsored professional development program. Remember those?

In those days companies really seemed to care about their employees and a once-popular measured metric called employee retention, which was the precursor to the modern-day employee engagement metric. Oddly enough, while employers still track employee retention, it's no longer discussed during board meetings and has been mostly relegated to a human resources measurement.

Employee retention programs were eventually renamed . . . *replaced* . . . with the much more pleasing-sounding "professional development programs." The purpose of these programs was an attempt to keep you around as an employee, to give you hope that there was another rung on the corporate ladder for you. Companies recognized your "local" expertise and did not want to lose you. They wanted to keep your CareerKred within their fours walls.

If you're smiling as you read that last sentence, you are not alone. In the years since the Great Recession, the local CareerKred environment has changed dramatically. Largely tied to our earlier discussion on efficiencies and reducing costs, in their quest to please "The Street," companies did away with employee retention and professional development programs as success metrics and instead decided to let you figure out your own career path—something for which none of us have been trained.

Today it's easier and less expensive for companies to hire for the role, not develop for potential. This mindset has largely been driven by the Internet and the rapid advancement of technology. As Taylor Pearson and I discussed in a recent podcast interview, it's much less expensive now for a company to hire your skill set at a lower wage from someone thousands of miles away with similar degrees and experiences.

My guess is you've probably seen this very thing happen within your company. Jobs have been outsourced overseas, or open positions within the company—especially senior level positions—have been filled by people from outside the company.

The Internet and advancing technologies will only accelerate this trend. Artificial intelligence algorithms will one day replace jobs that were once considered "sacred" within a company. When this happens, no jobs will be safe.

All of this is to say that the career formulas and paths you once knew, the ones that would help you advance locally, have become obsolete. You need a new path, one that is designed with the new career environment in mind. You require a path that allows you to chart your own course, choose you own adventure, and decide what you want to become known for.

To do this you must not only begin to think and act like a brand and a business of one, but you must also begin to think globally.

Think Globally

To advance in today's career environment, you must think globally. The very same forces that created the outsourcing trend are also the very forces that can free you from the old-school career path. If you're willing to accept the concept of CareerKred, that is.

As you might imagine, earning your CareerKred is a lot different today than it was a few years ago, and this is a very good thing for us in terms of branding. For starters, we can now earn CareerKred globally. Between the Internet and social media, we now have the ability to establish our expertise in a way that will resonate with people on the other side of the world, without showing them an old-school paper resume.

The Internet and social media have given job seekers and career-minded professionals the greatest career gift possible when it comes to earning CareerKred. Both the Internet and social media, if used intentionally and correctly, can make people and opportunities seek you out for your expertise.

But there is a "dark side" to the Internet and social media as well. You see it in the news every week. Some numbskull posts something online about his boss or his work hours and gets fired for it. You can also see it in every politically charged post online via Twitter or Facebook.

And while it may very well be your "right" to post whatever you want online, you do need to be prepared to get passed over for a job or miss some other opportunity you may be seeking because you choose to post something objectionable online.

Whether you like it or not, people judge you and make decisions about you based on what they find online. With every post you write, picture or video you upload, you leave behind a digital footprint for the entire world to see.

There are those who proclaim that they don't want to put themselves "out there" and thus refuse to embrace the concepts we'll discuss in this book. If this is your belief, I want you to read the next sentence carefully.

You already have an online presence, whether you want one or not.

Think about it. Do you have an account on any social media sites? (This includes Facebook, Twitter, LinkedIn, Google+, Instagram, Snapchat, etc.) Have you ever commented on a blog post, contributed to an online discussion, created a profile to donate to a cause, or been mentioned by others in any of the above items? If so, you have an online presence.

If you answered no to all of those questions, then you have, at least to this point, achieved invisibility online. But before you congratulate yourself, understand that, with a few quick keystrokes in the Google search bar, recruiters and hiring managers can find candidates within seconds for their open positions.

Care to guess what happens when they type your name in the search bar if you have no online presence?

If you're invisible, they move on. If, on the other hand, you do turn up in a search and what is displayed aligns with what the recruiter is looking for, you might just receive a call for an opportunity you didn't even apply for.

Think and Act like a Consultant

In today's global career environment, in addition to having a defined digital brand, you must also begin to think of yourself as a consultant versus an employee.

To boost your CareerKred today, you must think bigger. You must think beyond the scope of your role at your company. Think beyond the title you've been given and consider the skills and experiences you've gained during your career and how you can apply them as the brand of you . . . as a business of one . . . as a consultant, selling your skills and services to the highest bidder.

This book would never exist if I had continued to play the "head down, do your work" game. And believe me, I played that game. I was good at that game, because it was the only game in town.

My guess is that you are good at the game as well. But the fact that you picked up this book tells me that you are looking for something more for both your life and your career.

The good news is that this book will allow you to skip ahead about five years, which is how long it took me to learn the lessons you'll find within these pages. Together we'll walk through the steps required to build your CareerKred to a place where you will be noticed—not just locally but globally as well.

But to get there, you have to think bigger than you do today. You have to come out from the shadows of invisibility. You have to see yourself as a business of one. Whether you are an employee, a freelancer, a side business owner, or a full-fledged entrepreneur, building your CareerKred starts with a very simple concept.

You are a brand.

Chapter 9

The DICE Process

"Developing your personal brand is the same thing as living and breathing your résumé." —Gary Vaynerchuk

When I heard the words, "Ryan, you didn't get the position," I didn't realize my CareerKred was at an all-time low. But I did realize that I had two choices: continue down the same path or figure out a solution to move forward. That day I decided it was time to try a different path. Red pill, please.

That decision led to another, and another, and another, until eventually I discovered personal brands, personal branding, and the importance of developing and maintaining CareerKred. That single decision opened a new world of possibilities to me. Possibilities I didn't even know existed because they couldn't be seen from the well-worn path.

As I continued on my new journey, I picked up new skills along the way. I learned how to assess my strengths, how to define my brand, how to build websites, how to a start blog, and most importantly, why this stuff is important anyway.

I learned how to stand out from the crowd, become more visible, get recognized for my expertise, and how anyone, with enough hard work and effort, can use today's technology to impact his or her career.

Continuing down this path, I started to ask myself how could I help others do the same. Reflecting on this question, I noticed that everything I was blogging about, talking about, and learning about lived in three circles: personal brands, online reputation management (digital brand), and careers.

For the longest time, I saw these three circles as separate. Then one day, in a caffeinated state of awareness, it occurred to me that the three circles overlapped like a big Venn diagram. And at the center of this overlap was the process I now call DICE.

DICE is the formula I created for building your brand and boosting your CareerKred in today's digital-first world. It will help you grow an audience, become visible online, and gain recognition for your accomplishments and expertise.

As you probably guessed, DICE is an acronym. It represents a four-step process that includes Define, Integrate, Create, and Engage. For the remainder of this book, we will walk through this process step-by-step.

Overview of DICE

I mentioned it earlier but it bears repeating: For you to really grasp the concepts in this book, you must understand that each of us are a business of one. We are not employees. We are consultants selling our services, our skills, our traits, our training, and our expertise to the highest bidder.

Over the years I have watched the hiring process switch from one where individuals were hired based on resumes and interviews to one where an individual's skills are now assumed, and that person's ability to demonstrate those skills and expertise (CareerKred) in the public eye has become the deciding factor between him or her and all other candidates.

So how does the DICE process help you build CareerKred? It all starts by defining your brand.

Define

"Strong people define themselves; weak people allow others to define them." —Ken Poirot

We often compare ourselves to others, and this is especially true in our careers. Unconsciously, we equate our success with the success we see in others. In order to define YOUR brand, you must stop comparing yourself to others and begin to recognize the value you add and how you make a difference.

The Define step is not easy. It is the biggest section in this book for a reason. It's about asking hard questions of yourself, determining the value you add in the world, and identifying how you make a difference. It's about discovering your strengths and learning to focus on them instead of trying to fix your weaknesses.

More than anything, the Define step requires self-awareness. Self-awareness is having a solid understanding of who you are and how you relate to the world. Self-awareness is about being mentally and emotionally present in situations and understanding how you can best contribute.

It's also about being clued in to what you truly like and dislike.

Make no mistake: The Define step is real, hard work. Unfortunately, many people I work with want to skip this step. Why? Because it's not sexy, it requires introspection, and it can take a while to wrap your head around it. But here is my warning to you based on my experiences with clients:

People who skip this step will never live up to their full potential.

The Define step lays the groundwork for the rest of the DICE process. If you skip it, your branding efforts will fall short. You will not earn CareerKred because you will not understand how to link your strengths to what you want to become known for. You will not be ready for the next step in the process, the one everyone wants to skip right to: Integrate.

Integrate

Let me reiterate that you cannot successfully integrate yourself online if you don't know what you want to be known for. Why? Because the Integrate step is all about telling the world who you are and how you add value to it. This is what people want to find when they search for you online. They do not want to find pictures of the party you attended last weekend. At least most people don't.

We live in a digital-first age.

This means that your first encounter with hiring managers, recruiters, or potential customers (you can even add potential boyfriends and girlfriends here) will more than likely happen online. That's why it's so important for you to have a platform you, not Google, control, one where you can demonstrate your expertise.

The Integrate step isn't to be done willy-nilly or taken lightly. Your online profile, your digital brand, is the de facto resource people will use to judge you before they ever meet you in person. And let's face it, we all judge others by what we find online. Why should someone judging you be any different?

Posting pictures of kittens, puppies, and parties online will not gain you a spec of CareerKred, no matter how hilarious or entertaining they might be—unless, of course, kittens, puppies, and parties are your thing. The Integrate step is about strategically crafting your online presence, taking the brand you uncovered in the Define step and putting it online for all to see.

The Integrate step starts with a Google search for your name. Have you ever done this before? Judging by what I see posted online, I'd venture to say that many people haven't. Every day, people, maybe even you, post pictures of stupid crap, or sign up for the latest social media "thing," only to abandon it after a day, a week, or a month. If this is you, please stop now.

This behavior leaves you with an online presence so scattered that no recruiter, hiring manager, potential customer, boyfriend, or girlfriend will ever pursue you. In the discerning eyes of a recruiter, you will come across as not professional, and you will quickly become lost in the crowd and passed over.

The Integrate step, when done correctly, helps you tell your story online in a way that allows your CareerKred to shine and makes you standout from the crowd so people take notice. It ensures that when you are found in a search, you show up for whatever it is you want to be known for.

At a high level, the Define and Integrate steps are designed to help others get to *know* you. But for people to start to like you, you will need to give them a reason beyond just showing up in a search result. Which is why the next step of the DICE process is Create.

Create

"Don't tell people your dreams, show them."
—Anonymous

Create can be a challenging step, but it's a really important part of the process for boosting your CareerKred. Its purpose is to get people to like you—or not. You'll find out more what I mean by that last part a little later, but for now consider that it's OK if people don't like you during this step. In fact, it's almost desired.

Stepping out of your comfort zone during the Create step is also required. Shannon L. Alder once said, "Life always begins with one step outside of your comfort zone."[4] I understand now that when I heard the words, "You didn't get the position," it was largely because I had stopped pushing the boundaries of my comfort zone. I had become comfortable and complacent. As a result, my CareerKred had been diminished.

The Create step will change all this for you.

The Create step is you telling the world who you are and how you add value by creating content in your area of expertise for others to consume. In large part, this means you will share your thoughts in public.

The best way to create content is to start blogging. The preferred method is to do this on a website you own and control, but there are other methods as well, and later we'll discuss the pros and cons of each. Having your own place on the Internet is a critical part of the Integrate step.

For many of you, blogging will be difficult at first. This will be especially true if you haven't taken the time to Define what you want to be known for. The Define step is so important to the Create step that if you skip it, you will not be able to move forward in the DICE process.

Creating content in your area of expertise will most likely begin with writing. This is where all of my content creation starts. In addition to writing, other types of content you will create might include images, audio, and video. I view all of these as a pyramid, with one stacked on top of the other. Writing is at the base of the pyramid; it serves as the foundation. In terms of sophistication, it's the easiest to execute because it only requires your brain and some writing tools. The other content types sit on top of written content, and we'll discuss each in detail in the Create section of this book.

The content you create in this step will act as a magnet, repelling those who don't like your thoughts, insights, and ideas, and attracting those who do. This magnet helps people know where you stand; it

---

4 Alder, S. GoodReads.com. Quotes by Shannon Alder. Retrieved from http://www.goodreads.com/quotes/736100-life-always-begins-with-one-step-outside-of-your-comfort.

gives them an idea of who you are, how you think, and what you're about. Based on your content, people will either like you or not.

If they don't like your stance or your thoughts, they will move on to someone else—and this is a good thing. The Create step is the key to providing insight into you as a person or potential employee. This is what helps companies determine cultural fit.

Once you've used your content to tell the world who you are and how you add value, you'll move into the final step in the process, Engage.

Engage

By the time you get to the Engage step, you have defined your brand and what you want to be known for. You have strategically integrated your brand online in a way that will highlight your CareerKred, and you've started sharing your thoughts and expertise online.

As a consultant, as a business of one selling your services to your customer (i.e., employer), it is important for people to get to know, like, and trust you in order for them to do business with you. At this point in the DICE process, you have given anyone searching for you online all the reasons they need to know and like you. The Engage step will help you build trust.

There is no mystery to the Engage step. It is exactly what you think it is. It's reaching out to like-minded peers to build your network within your industry and outside of it. You'll do this by engaging with them via social media, meet ups, or even a good old-fashioned phone call.

The Engage step requires direct interaction with the audience you have built or are trying to reach. This interaction will help you build trust with people who can further help you grow your CareerKred. Ultimately, the Engage step will have an impact on your career.

At this stage of the DICE process, it's important for your message to remain consistent. You've worked yourself to a point where people trust you, which means they expect certain topics and conversations from you. This doesn't mean you can't go "off-brand" occasionally, but to do that, you need to have earned trust by following all of the steps in the DICE process.

Hopefully, you can see how the DICE process works at a high level. Of course, within each step there are a host of little steps and important details that will need to be implemented or at least considered before we move on.

Speaking of moving on, I'm ready to get going, aren't you? If so, I offer some final words of wisdom to help you get into the right mindset.

Some will follow you and some won't. But somewhere out there, someone is waiting for you and your message. Wouldn't it be a shame to deny that person (company or client) the benefit of your wisdom?

So if you're ready, let's go!

Part Three

The Define Step

"Too many people overvalue what they are not and undervalue what they are." —Malcolm Forbes

Uncover and define your brand today,
so others don't do it for you.

Digital Brand Assessment Score: 0—25 (35)

The "typical" assessment taker with a score between zero and twenty-five is firmly entrenched in the define step. Do you remember the song by Kenny Loggins in the movie *Top Gun*? If you find yourself here after taking the assessment, you are in the danger zone.

Most people in this range are oblivious about their personal and digital brands. Many have never even thought about their brand or why it matters. Finding them online is very difficult for recruiters, employers, or anyone else for that matter.

It's highly possible that opportunities are passing you by without you even knowing it. Here are some common traits for those who find themselves with a score in this range.

1. They are not aware of their brand.
2. They do not know how to get started defining their brand.
3. They have no presence online (digital brand) to speak of.
4. They do not know their real strengths.
5. They don't know what they want to be known for.

It's possible you have one or more of these traits. If so, it's OK. You are not alone. Many people feel the same way. The good news is that the Define step will help you replace these traits with new ones.

NOTE: No doubt you noticed the number thirty-five in parenthesis. If you have a unique name, it's possible for your score to creep up to thirty-five. A unique name makes you more easily found in a Google search, which will boost your score. But if you have a unique name and the descriptions above fit you, then the Define Step is the exact right place for you.

Chapter 10

What Do You Want to Be Known For?

You've probably heard this question before: "What do you want to do for the rest of your life?" That's a heavy question, and dare I say there are very few of us who can answer it with conviction.

The better question to ask yourself is: "What do you want to be known for?"

Why is this better? It's better for two reasons. First, it's easier to answer. This question is not as "heavy" as asking about the rest of your life.

Second, this question is nimble enough that your answer can change (and should) along with your circumstances.

Keep in mind, if you don't know what you want to be known for, how can you expect others to know? As Jane Anderson told us earlier, we often know what we *don't* want, but we have a hard time articulating what we *do* want.

You cannot build CareerKred without knowing what you want to be known for.

The entire DICE process relies on your ability to answer this question so you can direct all of your actions and energies toward this goal. I can't stress how important this is for you to understand. Take a minute right now and think about it. What DO you want to be known for?

If you're like most of my clients, my guess is you will struggle to answer this question. The reason you struggle is very simple. It's because you've never really taken the time to think about it. You've been so busy climbing that fictitious corporate ladder that you've never stopped to ask yourself if your career *direction* aligns with your career *aspirations*.

At some point in your career, you will start to question your choices, your decisions, and your path. When this happens, you feel stuck, maybe even trapped. You start to dread your commute to work, and Sunday evenings feel like a dementor from a Harry Potter book is slowly sucking the life out of you as look to the week ahead.

If this describes you, the good news is that you can get out of this funk. The bad news that is you can't get out of it without effort. But if you really want to unleash your Patronus Charm and chase away the Sunday evening dementors, you need to know the following three things about yourself.

1. Who you are
2. How you add value
3. What you want to be known for

To get to this point, you must understand your personal brand.

Personal Brand versus Personal Branding

"If you give me six hours to chop down a tree, I will spend the first four sharpening the axe." —Abraham Lincoln

What is personal branding? It's a question I hear all the time—on Twitter chats, on blog posts, and in person. What *is* personal branding?

Unlike those who look at your personal brand and personal branding in the same light, I keep the two terms separate. Based on my experience, I feel it is more accurate to look at them as two separate entities. First, there is your personal brand. Then, there is personal branding.

You cannot have the second without the first.

Your Personal Brand

Your personal brand is YOU. It's who you are at your core. It's your strengths, your values, your skills, your traits—it's who you are in the eyes of others. Hence, Jeff Bezos' comment that your brand is what others say about you when you are not in the room. How many times in the corporate world do you think people—hiring managers and human resources especially—say stuff about you when you're not in the room?

Ultimately you can't "control" what others think about you, but you can influence their perception by projecting the brand you want to be known for, which is where personal branding comes into play.

Personal Branding

Personal branding is the intentional act of telling the world who you are and how you add value. Pay special attention the word *intentional.* In the not so distant past, this used to be done locally through in-person interactions. Today personal branding is done globally through our intentional online presence and interactions in our digital-first world.

Matthew Capala, SEO expert, podcast guest, and founder of Alphametic, tells us that "80 percent of consumers search online before they buy."

Therefore, if you are a brand (a business of one), eight out of ten recruiters, hiring managers, and potential customers will look you up online *before* they decide to invest any time with you. That's why personal branding is so important—and why it's possible for you to make a first impression even while you sleep.

We'll talk a lot more about personal branding during the Integrate step, but for now know this: You will suck at *personal branding* unless you understand your *personal brand* first. Defining your personal brand before developing your personal branding is the same as Abe Lincoln spending the first four hours sharpening his axe before chopping down the tree. Unfortunately, I see too many people grab the axe and start chopping without even knowing what tree they want to cut to down.

As the saying goes, if all you have is an axe, everything looks like a tree. Following this approach you will make a dent in the tree, or maybe several trees, but eventually you will need to stop once the axe is dull.

Define Step 1

Chapter 11

Self-Awareness

"Self-awareness is being able to accept your weaknesses while focusing all of your attention on your strengths."
—Gary Vaynerchuk

Defining your brand requires you to become self-aware. Do you struggle with the term *self-awareness*? It wouldn't surprise me if you did; self-awareness is one of those terms that gets batted around a lot, especially in start-up and entrepreneurial circles.

According to Merriam-Webster.com, self-awareness is "knowledge and awareness of your own personality or character."

Another, more specific definition can be found at pathwayto happiness.com:

> [Self-awareness is] having a clear perception of your personality, including strengths, weaknesses, thoughts, beliefs, motivation, and emotions. Self Awareness allows you to understand other people, how they perceive you, your attitude and your responses to them in the moment.[5]

Combining the two, self-awareness is simply the self-knowledge of your personality/character that comes from taking into account your strengths, beliefs, motivations, and how you are perceived by others.

---

5 Van Warmerdam, G. *Self Awareness*. Retrieved from http://pathwaytohappiness .com/self-awareness.htm.

Why does understanding yourself matter so much? Because self-awareness will help you know where you add the most value, and it will help you improve your communication with others. Improved communication enables you to influence people and situations to get the results you desire, which in turn boosts your CareerKred.

Self-awareness is the starting point that leads to every improvement in your life and career. Interestingly enough, self-awareness is not new. It goes back as far as Socrates, who is credited for having said, "Know thyself," and it was discussed at length in Napoleon Hill's book *Think and Grow Rich*, first published in 1928.

Knowing yourself is difficult and takes hard work. It's a journey, but if you take it seriously, self-awareness is really the beginning of a lifetime growth and learning. Being self-aware will make it much easier for you to step out of your comfort zone in order to learn new behaviors or skills. It's during the moments you choose to be a bit uncomfortable that you have the most potential to learn and grow.

I hear you asking already: "If self-awareness is so important, how do you become more self-aware?"

Good question. Unfortunately, there is no specific formula or test you can take to become immediately self-aware. This is because we are all unique individuals. What works for me may not work for you.

However, what follows are the methods I have used to help my clients become more self-aware. These are the key tenets of the Define step.

The methods I use with my clients include introspection, observation, trusted advisors, and assessments. I personally needed to use all those methods to build my self-awareness in order to become comfortable with my brand. You may find as you go through the exercises that one or two of them is enough for you. However, speaking from personal experience, completing all four steps will help you define a more comprehensive brand in the end.

Defining your brand may be the hardest step in DICE process. Your success in the Define step will be based on your efforts. In other words, you get out of it what you put into it, because as it turns out, defining your brand is a solo game: you against yourself.

YOU must implement these methods. YOU must decide which method works best for YOU, and YOU must complete the exercises. So if you're ready, let's begin by looking at the least expensive, most basic method to begin understanding your brand: introspection.

Introspection

"Knowing yourself is the beginning of all wisdom." —Aristotle

Introspection is the examination or observation of your own mental and emotional processes. While it is the most basic method from an implementation standpoint, introspection might also be the most challenging.

Introspection requires YOU to pay attention to yourself by taking note of your experiences, your emotions, your actions, and your reactions in different situations. These notes, either mental or written, are an invaluable source of information about who you are and what makes you tick.

Practicing introspection requires you to pay attention to how you feel as you go through your days and weeks.

I realize that some of you may find the following exercise a little "hokey." However, recognizing how you "feel" in certain situations and acknowledging those feelings will give you insight into your brand. No one can feel these emotions for you. A coach can help coax them out of you, but YOU have to acknowledge them.

Exercise 2—Introspection

To help you become more self-aware, I have compiled a few questions for you to reflect on as you go about your day and week. To make the most of these questions, try to capture your answers as they happen.

I recommend using the associated worksheet for this exercise to write down your findings. You can download the worksheet at http://careerkredbook.com/workbook. Alternatively, you can write things down in a journal. Although not recommended, some of my clients make mental notes in their heads. Either way answering and acknowledging the feelings you experience during your week will help you shed light on your personal brand.

- Do you feel happier when working in a group or alone?
- How do you feel when you accomplish a difficult task?
- Is it easy or difficult for you to tell others what to do?
- When you start to feel bored and tired, what is going on around you?
- What is happening when you start to feel lively or interested?

As you can tell from the questions, introspection requires you to look at yourself objectively. This is very difficult for most of us to do because we are all naturally biased, but it's worth the effort. As you begin to look for answers to these questions, another important aspect of introspection, especially from a CareerKred standpoint, is to understand your skills and your traits.

BONUS: If you're someone who doesn't like to carry around a journal, another great way to capture your feelings through the week is to use your phone. Jane Anderson created an innovative app called Memo Mailer.

Once downloaded, you are greeted with a very simple user interface, a button. Press and hold the button while you dictate your emotions or thoughts. The app will record them and send them directly to your inbox. It's a simple and effective way for you to capture those moments as they are happening or shortly thereafter.

Traits and Skills

"Hire character. Train Skill." —Peter Schutz

Do you know the difference between your skills and your traits? Surprisingly a lot of people don't. Knowing the difference is especially critical when defining your brand. Let's take a minute to get clear on the differences between the two.

Traits

Traits, sometimes called attributes, are what make you different from other people. A trait is something that makes you *you*. It's the starting point of what people say about you when you're not in the room.

The expression, "Actions speak louder than words," is very true when it comes to a person's traits. We learn about who people are by watching how they interact with the world and paying attention to the way they treat others.

Traits consist of all the aspects of your behavior and attitudes that make up your personality and your character. We all have traits, both good and bad. Traits are a part of who you are, what you do, and why you do it.

Traits last a lifetime.

For fun, take a minute and think about your all-time favorite teacher. Now describe this person using only three words. Can you do it? The words you come up with to describe this person will more than likely be a list of his or her essential traits—such as being compassionate, calm, helpful, or kooky.

The challenge with traits, as with most of the things we explore during the Define step, is the fact that there are a countless number of traits you can identify in others, but it becomes a tad more difficult to identify the same number of traits in yourself.

Traits relate to your underlying values and beliefs. They often show up as descriptive adjectives, such as patient, unfaithful, religious, honest, loyal, loud, or jealous. Hence the reason your all-time favorite teacher may have been thoughtful, compassionate, and fun.

Skills

The flip side of traits is skills. Skills are learned. Generally speaking, skills are technical in nature, and just as you can learn them, you can forget them too.

Skills are the things you learn that enable you to perform certain tasks. Skills are the competencies you've acquired throughout your career and are required to perform specific tasks for your job. Your ability to execute on your skills is a critical part of building your CareerKred, especially in the early days of your career.

Skills are the things your boss most likely bases your performance review on.

If you're struggling to separate skills and traits, think of skills as action verbs. They include things like leading, delegating, coaching, paying attention to details, speaking a foreign language, handling customer complaints, managing suppliers, having good writing skills, communicating clearly, and even using a software program such as MS Project.

Exercise 3—Skills and Traits

In this exercise, you will identify your skills and traits. You will need the Exercise 3 worksheet to complete this exercise. You can find it in the *CareerKred Workbook* at http://careerkredbook.com/workbook. For reference, I have included a list of potential skills and traits here to help get you started.

First, review the lists for both traits and skills. Select five traits and five skills you believe you are known for today. Write these down on the first page of the worksheet.

Next, using the same list, select the top five skills and traits you believe *others* know you for today. Consider your peers, coworkers, bosses, and customers. What would they say your top skills and traits are? Write down these on the first page of the worksheet.

It may not seem like it now, but this will be important later in the Define step.

A note here on the lists: Neither the skills nor the traits listed are meant to be exhaustive. They are common ones designed to get you thinking. Feel free to Google *skills* or *traits* to find additional ones if you feel the ones on this worksheet are limited.

SKILLS - EXAMPLES

This is not an exhaustive list. The examples are provided to get you started. Feel free to search Google for additional skills not listed here.

CONSULTANT	QUICK RESULTS	PUBLIC SPEAKING	SIMPLIFY	ANALYSIS
TEAM BUILDER	CONSENSUS BUILDER	FACILITATOR	COACH	PRIORITIZE
GOOD W/ NUMBERS	THOUGH-LEADER	BUDGETING/ ESTIMATING	DECISION-MAKER	MOTIVATOR
DRIVE PRODUCTION	STRATEGY	WORKING WITH HANDS	PLANNING	CONTINUOUS IMPROVEMENT
TIME MANAGEMENT	MANAGE PEOPLE	TRAINER	MANUFACTURING	WRITER/EDITOR
PRESENTATIONS	PROJECT PLANNING	IDEATION/ BRAINSTORMING	PROBLEM SOLVER	VISIONARY
MENTOR	VOLUNTEER	ADVOCATE	NEW BUSINESS DEVELOPMENT	PROCESS-DRIVEN
DESIGNER/ GRAPHICS	IDEA-DRIVEN	LEADER	CONFLICT RESOLUTION	FUND RAISER
SALES	NEGOTIATION	MACHINE OPERATOR	ORDER TAKER	ADVISOR
RELATIONSHIP BUILDER	ORGANIZER	PROJECT MANAGEMENT	TEAM MEMBER	BUSINESS PLANNING
QUESTIONING	EXECUTE	CONNECTOR	LISTENER	ENABLER
COMMUNICATOR	OBSERVATION	DESIGNER	ARRANGER	

TRAITS - EXAMPLES

This is not an exhaustive list. The examples are provided to get you started. Feel free to search Google for additional traits not listed here.

POLISHED	IRRESPONSIBLE	HUMBLE	DIRECT	PROMPT
RELIABLE	QUIET	TOUGH	REALISTIC	RESOURCEFUL
ELOQUENT	FRUGAL	RESPONSIBLE	PERSISTENT	PASSIVE
THOUGHTFUL	PREDICTABLE	GOOD TEAM PLAYER	PLANS IN ADVANCE	CONFIDENT
APPROACHABLE	BIG PICTURE THINKER	RESPONSIVE	AMBITIOUS	GENEROUS
CREDIBLE	NEGATIVE	SELF-STARTER	CREATIVE	RESPECTED
WORKS ALONE	MICRO-MANAGER	INATTENTIVE	INNOVATIVE	GOOD LISTENER
EFFECTIVE	ACCOUNTABLE	DETAIL-ORIENTED	HELPFUL	LOUD
REASONABLE	FLEXIBLE	DELEGATES EFFECTIVELY	PRODUCTIVE	EMPOWERS
PATIENT	CAN DO ATTITUDE	INTEGRITY	PEOPLE PERSON	INDEPENDENT
POSITIVE	CAN'T DO ATTITUDE	SPONTANEOUS	ATTENTIVE	SHY/RESERVED
DETERMINED	CONNECTOR	RELATOR	FOCUSED	INFLUENCER
FUTURISTIC	ANALYTICAL	LEADER	STRATEGIC	

Transferable Skills

Before we move on, I want to quickly discuss transferable skills. For those considering a career change, understanding your transferable skills is, well, pivotal to your success.

If you are in the process of changing jobs, would like to move to a different field, or are trying to increase your CareerKred in a specific area, it's well worth the time to identify your transferable skills.

Transferable skills are your identified skills that can be transferred or leveraged from one job to the next. Transferable skills include leading, delegating, coaching, paying attention to details, speaking a foreign language, handling customer complaints, and managing suppliers.

All of these skills can be used in your next role. The challenge you face is recognizing them for what they are because, like skills, they are practically habits to you. You've been doing them for so long that they seem more like traits than skills.

So, as you assess new opportunities, identify not only your skills but also the skills that will transfer to a new role. These skills will play a critical part in helping you prepare for the position and for the hiring manager visualizing you in it. If you don't have the skills needed for a particular position, you will need to acquire them, which brings us to the next point I want to make about skills before moving on.

How Do You Obtain Needed Skills?

As you look to move into a new industry or new role, undoubtedly you will find some required skills that you do not possess. When you encounter this situation, you will not be able to relate these skills to your work experiences.

You have found what is commonly referred to as a "skills gap."

A skills gap is simply a gap between your current skills and the skills required for the role you are seeking. You will need to bridge this gap before you can make a change. This is especially true if you want to make a complete career change—for instance, from one specialty to another.

There are many ways you can obtain the skills to fill the gaps you've identified. Some will take longer than others to obtain. Here are a few suggestions.

- Go back to school and get a degree
- Take classes at a local vocational school
- Take course online at places, such as Lynda.com
- Volunteer for a leadership position
- Internships
- Apprenticeships

These are all legitimate ways for you to obtain necessary skills. Personally, I like volunteering because it accomplishes multiple things all at once. First, it demonstrates interest in the local community. Companies love to see this. Second, you can use your volunteer experience to develop skills you won't necessarily get the chance to develop working at your current company. For example, you may be able take a leadership position to further develop your leadership, organizational, and multitasking skills. Finally, volunteering provides you with the opportunity to network and demonstrate your skills to others within the organization.

Anyway you approach it, you will need to develop the skills where there are gaps in your experience. But knowing which ones you need to develop requires knowing what you want to do next—which why the DICE process begins with Define.

Your Values

"When your values are clear to you, making decisions becomes easier." —*Roy E. Disney*

Another piece of the self-awareness puzzle is understanding your values—specifically your work values. It may not seem important, but understanding your work values plays a big role in defining your brand. Whether you recognize them or not, you have values—values such as family, work, spiritual, leisure, and personal.

Your values help define who you are; they are the foundation for who you want to become. Your values embody what you believe is important about the way you live and work, the way you interact with customers.

Values are the goalposts—or the sidelines, if you prefer—for your life, your career, and your business. Your values determine your priorities.

They are the unconscious measures you use to determine if your life or business is turning out the way you want it to.

Values are that important, so we need to clearly define them.

From a career standpoint, your values help you determine cultural fit within a company. From a business standpoint, they tell you who you want to work with and how far you will go to help a client. When your values are out of alignment with what is happening with your career or your business, that's when things start to feel . . . *no bueno*.

That's why making a conscious effort to identify your values is vital to your brand. Placing yourself in an environment contrary to your values can cause you to change your behavior, which will ultimately rub your brand the wrong way.

Life and business are much easier when you acknowledge your values and make career or business decisions that honor them. The quickest way to dishonor your values is chasing money—for example, taking a job or client because it pays more whether or not it's the right fit for you.

Other examples include holding onto a job that requires you to work eighty hours in a week while one of your key values is family, or working in a highly competitive sales environment when you don't value competition.

I think you'd agree that, in either of these cases, you will not be very satisfied with your job.

In these types of situations, being clear about your values will help. When you know your values, you can use them to make decisions about your life and your career, decisions such as:

- What job should I pursue?
- Should I accept this promotion?
- Should I start my own business?
- Should I follow tradition or travel down a new path?

I can't state this enough: Understanding your values will help you determine the best direction to take when the way forward is uncertain.

The good news is that you've already answered several of the questions required to identifying your values. For the rest, you'll need to complete the following exercise.

Exercise 4—Identify Your Values

In this exercise, you will focus on and rank your work values. You will need the Values worksheet to complete this exercise. You can find it in the *CareerKred Workbook* at http://careerkredbook.com/workbook. For reference, I have included a list of potential Values to help get you started.

As you complete the values exercise, remember that your values will form the basis for your career and business decisions.

Using only a one, three, or five, review each value and give it a ranking. The number you assign to any particular value indicates its importance to you.

A five indicates a high level of importance. A three indicates the value is neither important nor unimportant, while a one indicates the value is not as important to you. Do not feel bad if you allocate a value as a one. There are no right or wrong answers; there are only *your* answers.

After you have assigned a number to each value, review the list again and make adjustments as necessary. Take a look at the top five values you've identified. Do they feel right to you? If so, write them down on the worksheet, and then let's move on.

WORK VALUES - EXAMPLES

The examples are provided to get you started. Feel free to search Google for additional Values not listed here. I've included at the end of the list space for you to add any additional values that are important to you.

Value	Description
Achievement	Ability to regularly meet or exceed annual goals and objectives
Advancement	Ability to be promoted to higher levels within the company
Autonomy	Be able to determine the nature of work without significant direction from others
Balance	Have a job that allows time for family, leisure, and work.
Challenge	Engage with complex questions and demanding tasks, troubleshooting and problem-solving.
Collaboration	Working with multiple people inside and outside the company on project teams
Commute	Length of time it takes to get the office location.
Compensation	Amount of salary including bonuses or other forms of payment
Creativity	Be able to express your creative ideas in the arts and communication
Community	Company is active in volunteering, politics, or service projects.
Decision Making	Have the power to decide courses of action, policies, etc or make decisions regarding the work activities of others.
Excitement	Experience a high degree of stimulation or frequent novelty and drama on the job
Fun	Have opportunities to be playful and humorous at work
Flexible work schedule	Work according to my time schedule, i.e. non-specific times or work from home.
Helping Others	Be involved in helping or being of service to people directly, either individually or in groups.

WORK VALUES - EXAMPLES

Value	Description
Helping Society	Contributing to the betterment of the world
Influence	Be in a position to influence attitudes or opinions of other people.
Job Security	Have a stable work environment and reasonable financial reward.
Job Satisfaction	Happy with role and career trajectory
Leadership	Direct, manage, or supervise the work done by others.
Leverage past experiences	Ability to use your past experiences in a new role
Location	Area to live in. Specifically the State, city and/or town
Moral or Spiritual Fulfillment	Feel that my work is consistent with my ideals or moral code.
Personal Growth	Have work which enables me to grow as a person
Prestige	Holding or having a position of high standing within an organization
Public Contact	Have a lot of day-to-day contact with people
Recognition	Get positive feedback and public credit for work well done.
Stability	Have a work routine and job duties that are largely predictable and not likely to change over a long period of time.
Teamwork	Have close working relations with group; work as team for common goals
Travel	Ability to travel for business.
Vacation or PTO	Amount of Paid time off
Variety	The ability to do different activities

Chapter 12

Observation

Strongly related to introspection, observation requires you to actively pay attention when certain situations present themselves. It requires identifying certain behaviors you demonstrate and the environment in which they occur. By doing so you'll capture factors such as who is involved or what just happened.

For any of your observations to offer objective information, they need to be specific and vivid in your mind, which is why I recommend capturing them using Jane's Memo Mailer app. Thinking back to the previous introspection questions, did you observe any of the following activities?

- A change in your body language
- Increased energy or animation
- Decreased energy or animation

For me, soon after I started my journey to build my brand and CareerKred, I started to notice that during meetings when people were describing a complex process, I would start shaking my leg. At the same time, I could feel a sense of energy building inside of me.

When I finally started "listening to it," I understood that the energy was telling me to stand up and begin facilitating the meeting. In many cases, it was specifically telling me to go to the whiteboard and map out the process.

Looking back, this had always happened; I had just never consciously observed it before.

The funny thing is that once you observe these behaviors in yourself, you can't *unobserve* them. Your traits, talents, or strengths are telling you to act in one way or another, to step up or step out.

One method that may help you with your observations is to keep a journal, just as with introspection. In your journal, write down events that took place during the day and how those events made you feel.

While journaling your day may seem a little compulsive to you, if you're really looking to understand how you make decisions, writing down what you believe to be the pros and cons of any given decision will help you recognize the feelings you associate with making decisions. While it may not seem like it now, observation will ultimately help you become more honest with yourself and your business.

As an example, maybe you've always dreamed of being a VP at your company or starting your own business. When you look at your career, you owe it to yourself to review your skills, traits, and values, and then ask yourself if you really have it in you to take on those roles. Do the requirements of the role—such as the hours you put in, the amount of travel, the presentations you give, the customer discussions and the expectations—really align with who you are?

Or is it possible that you might be more in love with the idea of those roles versus actually living up to the expected standards for them?

You have to take the time to audit yourself, because once you know yourself through introspection and observation, you may discover that the role you think you want is actually not the direction you should be heading. Taking that role may make you feel worse.

Sometimes we copy others because we think they live the life or have the job we want. But what we often don't consider is that we may not be wired in the same way as the person currently in that role. What works for someone else may not work for you.

Observation by itself is a very useful tool. However, it's also highly possible that it may only get you so far. So another method you can use as a part of your self-audit is to ask for the observations of others.

Trusted Advisors

"There is no lack of knowledge out there;
just a shortage of asking for help." —Anonymous

When was the last time someone told you, "I know you better than you know yourself?" Usually we hear this from someone close to us.

We typically brush off this statement quickly, but the reality is that when someone says those words to us, it's because he or she has observed us making similar decisions in similar situations in the past. It is quite possible the person actually does know us better than we know ourselves. That's why, in times of important decisions, we reach out to those we trust and ask for advice, suggestions, or help.

Why don't we do the same when it comes to our careers?

The truth is that many of us don't consider our peers as people who may in fact, know us better than we know ourselves. Think about it for a minute. Who knows better how you think and process information at work: your peers or your family?

At this point in the Define step, you need to take the time to reach out to those people around you—people you trust—and ask them about you. This will be difficult, and while it may be challenging, I'm going to suggest this may be the most eye-opening part of the Define step.

No matter how hard you try, there will be some behaviors you demonstrate that you will not be able to "see." You are simply too close to the action to catch them. This is why you need to speak with trusted advisors.

We all have trusted advisors. Chances are good that you may not recognize them as such, but these are the people you go to when you need help or advice when making a decision. These are the "I know you better than you know yourself" people—these are the people whose opinion matters to you.

They can include family, coworkers, and current or previous bosses. Their "title" does not matter. What's key here is that you trust them, take their advice seriously, and are willing to use their opinions (based on their observations) as a basis for your own decision-making process.

Your trusted advisors provide you with the validation you need as you continue to define your brand.

Trusted advisors help you gain additional insights into your brand, so don't be surprised if their insights surprise you. Asking your trusted advisors for their thoughts about you is where the "rubber hits the road," so to speak. It's where the perceptions you hold for yourself run smack into the perception of others.

From a CareerKred standpoint, the perception of others can either serve as a limiting factor or the greatest acceleration factor in your career. That perception makes the difference between hearing, "You got the job" or "You didn't get the job."

Through interactions with your trusted advisors, you have been building a perception in their minds. Some of your trusted advisors know you so well, they can describe your brand to a "T," and it's for this exact reason that we reach out to them and ask, "What do you know me for?"

Hearing someone else answer this question, especially someone whom you trust, can be eye-opening and very empowering.

Going back to the VP role example, it could be that the one thing holding you back is the romantic version of who you think you are versus who you actually are. The observations and opinions of your trusted advisors can, and usually do, provide you with a healthy dose of reality.

Some of my clients have struggled with the answers they get back from their trusted advisors. Not because they are "wrong," but because the answers run counter to their thought process.

If this happens to you, you may doubt your advisors' authenticity, initially thinking and even saying out loud, "They are just telling me what they think I want to hear." If you think this way, you've chosen the wrong people to ask.

I can tell you from personal experience that hearing directly from others about what they think you are good at and not so good at is necessary for personal and professional growth. It's a key to becoming self-aware and developing your CareerKred.

If you do receive some "negative" feedback from a trusted advisor, it's important for you to keep the big picture in mind during the Define step, which involves defining yourself—perhaps for the very first time.

Author's note: As you progress through the Define step, it's important to keep in mind the insights you are gaining through introspection, observation, and soon from your trusted advisors all serve as data points that you—and you alone—must assemble in a manner that makes sense to you.

Exercise 5—Your Trusted Advisors

For this exercise, select at least ten people whose opinions matter to you. Once you've selected your trusted advisors, you are going to send them an email and ask for their help. If the feedback you receive suggests you need to change your behavior, career direction, or even the way you dress, promise yourself that you will give the advice serious consideration.

The script on the next page is the exact script I use. I've provided it here as an example. Feel free to use it as is, or change it up to "make it your own."

You may feel a bit apprehensive asking for this information, and that's OK; it's perfectly normal. Remember, discovering your brand requires you to ask uncomfortable questions and receive what may be uncomfortable answers.

After you send the email, allow five days to pass before you send any follow-up correspondence. Like you, your trusted advisers are busy, and they may require some additional time to process your request before they can provide you with the most valuable feedback. After five days with no response, though, go ahead and send a follow-up email.

Trusted Advisor Email Template

Dear (name here),

I recently started working with an executive coach to better understand "what difference I make." I have always appreciated your opinion, and because you are someone whose opinion matters to me, I'd appreciate your valuable feedback.

Can you please take a few minutes to reply to this email with a list of the top five words (personality traits and skills) or short phrases that you believe best describe what I am known for as it relates to your experience of knowing or working with me? Constructive feedback is as valuable as positive feedback, so do not hesitate to provide it if you feel it is applicable.

Please help me to identify five things I do (skills) and how I do them (traits) that occur to you when my name is mentioned in a professional context.

SKILLS (What I Do)

1.
2.
3.
4.
5.

TRAITS (How I Do It)

1.
2.
3.
4.
5.

I am grateful for your help and thank you in advance for providing these insights. I would like to have your response back by (insert date).

Thank you!

Chapter 13

Assessments

"Today you are You, that is truer than true. There is no one alive who is Youer than You."—Dr. Seuss

At this point, you might be looking for a little more of a "scientific" method to help you define your brand. This where assessments come into play. The right assessments can help you understand why you do the things you do, why you find certain tasks simple, and why you seem to "ride the struggle bus" with other tasks.

Assessments can help you understand your unique differences. Once you know what makes you unique, you can use these differences to your advantage in order to excel in your chosen profession—or help you choose your next one.

There are many different assessments available for you to take today. Some are free, while others can cost over fifty dollars. For my coaching clients, I recommend taking at least two of the following assessments:

- Strengths Finder 2.0
- StandOut
- Fascination Advantage
- 16personalities.com

Yes, I said at least two, and here's why. In my experience, if you take just one assessment, it will be easy for you to question the results. You'll try to rationalize or debunk what the assessment is telling you. However, if you take a second assessment, it will be harder for you to deny the results of the first one when you see firsthand how closely the two assessments correlate.

You will find that both assessments reinforce each other's results. The first assessment will be eye-opening for you. It will shed light on your talents and make you see yourself in a different manner. Maybe not right away, but you'll start to notice certain talents when they surface. But taking two or more assessments can be positively game-changing.

Assessments provide you with a scientific, unbiased methodology to help you understand where you fit in any organization and how you can add the greatest value. They are integral to gaining self-awareness.

I personally have taken multiple assessments, and this has helped me understand a great deal about where and how I work best. I've used the information from the assessments to analyze potential career opportunities and business opportunities that align with my strengths, my skills, and my traits.

How cool would it be to choose your next position based on what you know you excel at and are good at versus taking a position because someone else thinks you should? Or worse, taking a position for money?

To help you understand the assessments better, I've provided the following brief descriptions about what you can expect from each one.

StrengthsFinder 2.0

"The key to human development is building on who you already are" —Tom Rath

The granddaddy of them all, Gallup originally published StrengthsFinder in 1998. The assessment is a culmination of forty years of research conducted by Donald Clifton on human strengths.

You can buy the *StrengthsFinder 2.0* book on Amazon for around fifteen dollars. The book contains a code that allows you to take the assessment on the Gallup Strengths website.

There is one common misconception about the StrengthsFinder assessment that I want to address before we move on.

The assessment itself will not help you find your strengths. It helps you discover your natural talents. The idea behind the assessment is that once you know your natural talents, you can work on strengthening them so they eventually become your strengths. This might seem like semantics, but I see people struggle with this distinction every day.

I am often asked why should someone take the StrengthsFinder assessment. There are a variety of reasons, but I think Lisa Cummings, CEO of Pinch Yourself Careers and a Gallup Certified Strengths coach, summed it up best when she told me during our podcast interview:

> If you're struggling at work, if you're burnt out, if you're feeling drained by the work you do every day, then take the assessment. It can act as a rearview mirror so you can see how things—the responsibilities you have today, for example—can push you into your weakness zone. Knowing this will allow you to start to shape the job you're in so it can energize you instead of draining you.

These are powerful words, and they just might sum up the entire point of the Define step. Knowing who you are and what your natural talents are allows you to focus them on the things in life that energize you. During introspection, one of the tasks was to identify those times during the week when you felt energized or in the zone. Imagine if you could have that feeling every day at work?

Becoming self-aware moves you in that direction; the StrengthsFinder assessment will give the language you need to describe it.

What You Get

It takes about a half hour to complete the StrengthsFinder assessment. Honestly, there are a lot of questions—like 177 of them. But after you complete the assessment, you'll immediately get a report that spans nearly twenty pages. When you take the assessment, you'll get ranked for thirty-four possible talents, but your report will only provide you with the top five.

If you want to know what your remaining twenty-nine talent themes are, Gallup will provide you access to your full report for an extra $79. In my opinion, the top five are all you really need to get a good grasp on your talents.

Your report is divided into three sections: Awareness, Application, and Achievement.

Each section provides specific details about each of your top five talents. For example, the Awareness section contains a description, insights, and questions you can answer to help you become more aware of your talents.

A side effect of taking the assessment is that you will discover yourself throughout your workweek, noticing when you display your talents. And trust me, you will. Once you know your natural talents, you will not be able to unknow them.

For these reasons, I recommend taking the StrengthsFinder assessment. Understanding your top talents will provides you with some great insights into yourself as a person—and ultimately you as a brand.

However, there is one catch.

Gallup does not combine your results into one comprehensive answer that helps you understand how to interpret and use your results; they leave the interpretation up to you. This is both good and bad, but I've developed an exercise that will help you pull your talents together.

I've taken the StrengthsFinder exam three times now, and I can never really argue with any of the results. I display everything the Strengths-Finder assessment points out. In case you were wondering, my top five talents are: Strategic, Relator, Futuristic, Ideation, and Intellection.

This basically means that I love to solve problems with well-thought-out and logical solutions.

StandOut

"You'll grow most where you're already strong."
—Marcus Buckingham

I touched on it in the previous section, but we've all experienced days where we reach the end of the day and say out loud, "Wow. Today flew by!" Remember those days? Odds are that on those days you were using your natural talents. From Marcus Buckingham's point of view, those are the days when you "stand out."

Wouldn't it be nice if those days happened more often? They can if you understand what makes you stand out.

Marcus Buckingham first published the StandOut assessment in 2009. Mr. Buckingham worked with Donald Clifton at Gallup.

Yes that's right, the company that created the StrengthsFinder assessment.

I know what you're thinking. If the same guy who worked at Gallup and co-authored a book with the founder of StrengthsFinder, what is the difference between StrengthsFinder and StandOut?

This is a good question and one Mr. Buckingham addresses in detail in the introduction to the *StandOut* book. Although I'm sure it's technically incorrect, I view this assessment as a refinement of the StrengthsFinder assessment, yet at the same time, it builds on the research conducted by the StrengthsFinder team. I see the two as very complimentary.

At its core, StrengthsFinder provides you with language to describe yourself. It helps you begin to understand *you*. With the StrengthsFinder assessment, I struggled to answer these questions: What do you do with the information? Where do you go next?

The StandOut assessment seeks to answer these questions by providing you with suggestions for potential careers and tips on how you can "win" in various roles.

Instead of 34 talents, the StandOut assessment makes use of nine strength roles, *Advisor, Connector, Creator, Equalizer, Influencer, Pioneer, Provider, Stimulator, and Teacher.*

The StandOut assessment book is modeled after the StrengthsFinder book and provides a brief overview of the assessment, including the backstory of how the assessment was created. The bulk of the book details each of the nine strength roles.

What You Get

Plan on taking a half hour to complete the StandOut assessment. Once completed, you'll get a fifteen-page report that ranks and details your top two strength roles.

You'll also get details for each of your top strength roles combined. I found the combined strength roles, called "the comparative advantage," to be very interesting and unique. Unlike the StrengthsFinder assessment, with the "cost of admission" for the StandOut assessment you get to see how you ranked for the remaining strength roles in order.

Your strength roles are divided into multiple sections that include detailed insights such as:

- When you are your most powerful
- Phrases that describe you
- How to make an immediate impact
- How to take your performance to the next level
- What to watch out for

Having spent a lot of time reviewing and trying to understand my strengths, I found the StandOut assessment refreshing and full of applicable information. My top two strength roles are Advisor and Creator.

The Comparative Advantage

One of the things that makes this assessment unique is the combination of your top two strength roles into one comparative advantage. The comparative advantage provides you with additional insight not covered in each strength role. As an Advisor and Creator, for instance, my comparative advantage states: "You're a creative problem solver. You see the full picture and offer practical strategies for filling the gaps."

As with the individual strengths roles, the combined strength roles section details the same insights and matches your combined strengths with one another. In addition, the assessment goes one step further and tells you how to "win" or apply your strength roles as a leader, a manager, a client services representative, and a sales representative.

To me, this was the most powerful part of the assessment. It is what makes the StandOut assessment, in my opinion, stand out. Understanding how to apply your strengths roles is very empowering, and this assessment lays that out for you.

If you are interested in seeing what the StandOut report looks like, you can find my actual results at ryanrhoten.com/standout.

Fascination Advantage®

"Different is better than better." —Sally Hogshead

The Fascination Advantage assessment is one of my favorites. It's the one I recommend most often. To say that the Fascination Advantage® assessment is unique would be an understatement.

Most assessments, including the two already mentioned, are designed to help you look inside yourself so you can describe how you see the world. The Fascination Advantage® assessment, however, flips this traditional approach on its head by giving you insights on how the world sees you. It's a subtle but key difference, and it's why I like this assessment so much.

Invented by Sally Hogshead, the Fascination Advantage® assessment is a science-based personality brand measurement assessment. The assessment tells you how your personality is most likely to impress and influence the people you interact with on a daily basis.

It allows you to discover the best of yourself through the science of fascination and it does this by determining your personality advantages. The Fascination Advantage assessment breaks your personality down into seven distinct advantages: Innovation, Passion, Power, Prestige, Trust, Mystique, and Alert.

All of us have one primary advantage and one secondary advantage. Your advantages help you understand how you add value in any given situation.

What You Get

At the time of writing this book, the Fascination Advantage requires an investment of $47, making it the most expensive assessment I recommend. But it is money well spent. Your superpowers, as Sally calls them, are determined by answering twenty-eight questions in five to ten minutes. It's by far the shortest timeframe of all the assessments.

After you answer the questions, you receive an in-depth customized report that includes:

- A detailed description of your unique advantages
- Graphs and charts of your score analysis
- "Warnings" of how you could be turning people off
- The way in which you are least likely to fascinate
- Action steps and one-minute coaching
- Visual design and personalized videos

Your Fascination Advantage® report will define your unique advantages, both primary and secondary, as well as how to use them to propel your career. The fact that this assessment helps link your advantages to your career is pretty cool.

The Fascination Advantage® takes your personal advantages one step further by combining your primary and secondary advantage into one cohesive archetype. It does this by plotting your advantages with all seven advantages against a matrix to create forty-nine potential personality archetypes. Your archetype is a combination of your primary and secondary personality advantages.

My primary advantage is innovation. My secondary advantage is power. Together they combine to create my archetype as the Maverick Leader. If you're interested in taking this assessment, check it out at howtofascinate.com.

16personalities.com

I recently discovered 16personalities.com, and I must say, I really like it. Taking this assessment will give you a concrete, accurate description of who you are and why you do things the way you do. As a bonus, this assessment is free.

The test yields similar results to Myers Briggs, but does it in a more fun and meaningful way. It takes less than twelve minutes to complete, and all the questions are answered on a sliding scale requiring you to rank your agreement with the question. The scale goes from Agree to Disagree, and there are about seventy questions for you to answer. Did I mention the test is free?

What You Get

Once you've finished taking the test, you immediately get your results in the form an archetype. There are sixteen potential archetypes, or personalities (hence the name of the site), divided into four categories: Analysts, Diplomats, Sentinels, and Explorers. I fall into the Diplomat category as a Protagonist.

Your report is online so you can always find the descriptions of your archetype on the website, but if you provide an email address, you can have the report sent to you. The report covers seven areas:

1. Introduction
2. Strengths and Weaknesses
3. Romantic Relationships
4. Friendships
5. Parenthood
6. Career Paths
7. Workplace Habits
8. Conclusion

The free version of this personality test provides you with a surprising amount of personalized information. I found the career section to be particularly fascinating. All of the sections provide you with language you can actually use and understand.

I highly recommend checking it out. I promise you'll be amazed by how closely the results describe you.

Exercise 6—Take an Assessment . . . or Three

In this exercise, we're going to focus in on the core of your brand. You will need the Exercise 6 worksheet for this exercise. You can find it in the *CareerKred Workbook* at http://careerkredbook.com/workbook.

To complete this exercise, you will need to take at least one assessment. It doesn't matter which one, but I recommend that you start with the free one at 16personalities.com.

Read through the results of the assessment. Highlight any phrases that stand out in your mind. It's important to capture only the phrases that make you stop and say, "Yes, that's me!"

Do this for each assessment you take. Don't think about how the phrases go together yet; just highlight the sentences that resonate. It's important to complete the worksheet because it will be used later to help you draft your summary and tagline.

After you've completed the worksheet, set the assessments aside and focus only on the worksheet you've just completed. Read over the phrases you highlighted. Let them sink in.

For the next few days, take some time to observe your behavior. As you go about your day and your workweek, you'll notice when you display a behavior specified by the assessment, because as I said before, once you know your strengths, you will not be able to unknow them.

Define Step 2

Chapter 14

The Future You

We've discussed some pretty heady stuff to this point. If you've been doing the exercises, you now know more about yourself than ever before. You understand your talents, your skills, your traits, and maybe even more depending on which assessment you decided to take. You did take one, right?

What we haven't discussed, however, is the critical component to your success in the next step of the process. Without knowing this, even with everything you now know about yourself, you will not be successful in the Integrate step. It's time to talk about what it is you want to be known for.

If you could start your career over and do anything you wanted, what would you do? Hopefully it would be something that brings you enjoyment and fulfills you. Most importantly, I hope it's something that allows you to use your natural talents.

To help you get to this point, take a few minutes and complete the following exercise.

Exercise 7—Define the Future You

In this exercise, you will take an in-depth look at what we'll call "the future you." You will need the Future You worksheet for this exercise. You can find it in the *CareerKred Workbook* at http://careerkredbook.com/workbook.

The Future You exercise will be the basis for discovering what you want to be known for. On the worksheet titled "Future You," you will answer a series of questions. All the questions are designed to get you to consider your future possibilities.

In order for this to work as designed, you'll need to reference the worksheets you've already completed.

I think you will find this exercise very enjoyable since you have worked through all of the other exercises.

Complete the worksheet for this exercise and keep it close. You'll be referencing it again soon.

Define Step 3

Chapter 15

Personal Brand Statement (Tagline)

One of the questions I ask in the digital brand assessment is "What are you currently struggling with when it comes to your brand?" The question may seem nebulous, but the answers I get back are priceless.

For those whose score puts them in the Define step, one of the most common pieces of feedback I receive relates to not understanding how to describe themselves succinctly. This is where having a personal brand slogan or tagline comes in handy.

A personal brand statement or tagline is not a necessity, but it can help. Think of those times when you've been asked to describe yourself. At that moment, a personal brand tagline would be a good thing to use as your answer.

Before we get started building your personal brand statement, keep in mind that a personal brand statement has more than a few aliases. I've mentioned a couple already, such as tagline or slogan. Both of these are aliases for a personal brand statement. I'll use these terms interchangeably since they essentially describe the same thing.

So, what is a personal brand statement? Regardless of what you call it, at a high level a personal brand statement is a phrase that provides you with a way to succinctly summarize who you are and how you add value.

Done correctly, it can also provide a creative way for you to be remembered.

In order for it to work as designed, your personal brand statement should be easy to remember, it should place your brand front and center, and it should emphasize your CareerKred. Taglines have an innate ability to help you leave behind a piece of yourself after you've left the building, so to speak.

According to Google, a *tagline* is "a catchphrase or slogan, especially as used in advertising."

As you may recall from earlier, personal branding is the intentional act of telling the world who you are and how you add value. And per Google's answer, I'm sure you'd agree that your personal brand tagline is a very basic form of advertising.

Interestingly enough, a *slogan* is defined as "a short and striking or memorable phrase used in advertising."

Combining these definitions, your personal brand statement becomes a short and striking catchphrase that conveys to your audience who you are and how you add value.

Which begs the question: Why on earth would you want a tagline for your brand anyway?

Why Build a Personal Brand Statement?

Does a personal tagline seem silly to you? It did to me at first too. Then I took a step back and asked myself, "If I had a personal brand statement, when in the last year would I have used it?"

Here are some reasons that may resonate with you:

1. Introductions at conferences or networking events
2. Whenever someone asks, "What do you do?"
3. Whenever someone said, "Tell me about yourself."

Can you think of any other occasions where a personal brand tagline could come in handy?

In addition to being a quick and concise way to communicate who you are and how you add value, a personal brand statement can also act as a confidence booster for you.

A confidence booster? Absolutely. Think about the last time you had to tell others about yourself. How did you answer? Did you fumble over your words? Did you use your job title in your introduction? Whatever approach you took to answering the question, I'm guessing you quickly fizzled out. Not very confident, eh?

I'd also guess that five minutes later, people didn't remember what you said.

Having a personal brand statement will not only provide you with a conversation starter, but if done correctly, it can instill confidence in you, and this will be "felt" by the people who hear your response.

When you have a concise answer to the question "What do you do?", you will become more memorable in the eyes of others.

Components of Your Personal Brand Statement

Don't be intimidated by the idea of putting your personal brand statement together. Believe it or not, if you've been completing the exercises up to this point, you are much closer than you think. If you haven't yet done the work, you might want to go back to the start of the Define step before you continue. Each step in this process builds on the previous steps. Sorry, but you just can't skip ahead.

As you begin this exercise, think about the process of creating your personal brand statement as a big funnel. Everything you've completed so far serves as an input into this funnel. The inputs are in the form of the phrases you've collected for each assessment, your skills and traits, the feedback from your trusted advisors, the defined future you, and your values. Pour all these inputs into the top of your funnel.

We want to start this process with as much information about **you** as we can because together we will filter it all down into a concise and memorable phrase. When you are finished with this exercise, your personal brand statement will be one sentence that answers the following questions:

- I am—Who you are, the title you give yourself
- I help—Who do you add value to? (This is your audience.)
- I understand/do—How you add value to your audience
- So that—The type of transformation your audience should expect to receive

Exercise 8—Create Your Personal Brand Statement

To complete this exercise, you will need the Personal Brand Statement worksheet from the *CareerKred Workbook* at http://careerkredbook.com/workbook.

In addition, you will need all of the completed exercises from the workbook. Typically you will use your skills and traits as adjectives in your personal brand statement, while the phrases from your assessments and trusted advisors will make up the bulk of the finished statement. You will use your values as a double check for your personal brand tagline when finished.

To get started, on the Personal Brand Statement worksheet, fill in your top five values, skills, and traits from the previous worksheets. You might find this a little redundant, but I have found writing these things down again will help you remember why you selected them in the first place.

Once finished, move into the next section and write out the final phrases you identified at the end of the assessment worksheet as well as the top phrases from your trusted advisors. Now that you have your list of phrases, skills, traits, and values that best describe you, you're ready to take a stab at creating a first draft of your personal brand statement. You'll do this by combining and consolidating your inputs.

Before you write anything down, look for commonalities between the phrases you've identified. If you notice any, go ahead and combine them into one phrase or sentence.

Once you've combined similar sentences/phrases, it's time to narrow down everything from the first page into something more manageable. Keep in mind that you are moving down a funnel as you build your personal brand statement. If you have twenty sentences/phrases, for example, you should cut them down to ten without losing the jist of all twenty sentences.

You will repeat this a second and possibly even a third time.

The Personal Brand Statement Framework

By the time you've narrowed down your phrases three times, you'll probably think you can't narrow them down any further. Typically at this point, you'll have between three and five sentences. But we need to go deeper.

Your goal is to get to *one* sentence—one sentence that helps those who hear it understand who you are, who you help, and what you help those people understand or do so they can experience some type of transformation.

To get there you are going to rewrite your three to five sentences using this framework:

- I am
- I help
- Understand/do
- So that

I Am

This is the opening part of the statement. It is *not* your job title. For this part of the statement, think about what it is you are known for today or what you want to be known for tomorrow (the future you).

Do you want to be known as a personal branding specialist, podcast editor, product manager, speaker program manager? Whatever your thing is, this is the "I am" part of your statement. Here are a few examples:

I am a career coach.
I am a career branding strategist.
I am a digital branding specialist.

I Help

In order to build your brand and increase your CareerKred, you need to know who it is you help. Sticking with the previous examples, if you're a personal branding specialist, you might help Millennials, Gen Xers, Baby Boomers, etc. If you're a podcast editor, it seems natural that you would help your fellow podcasters, and as a speaker program manager, you help organizations or individuals.

Combining the "I am" and "I help" framework together gives you the following:

I am a career coach; I help executives . . .
I am a career branding strategist; I help career coaches . . .
I am a digital branding specialist; I help recruiters . . .

Understand/Do

The third part of your personal branding statement is where the excitement begins. This is where you tell your audience—those people you've just identified as those you help—what exactly it is you help them understand or do.

As a personal brand specialist, you might help Gen Xers define and build their brand. A podcast editor most likely collects audio files, edits them, and uploads them to a hosting service for their audience. A speaker program manager may help organizations find and book speakers for upcoming events.

Combining "I am" and "I help" with the Understand/Do framework together gives you the following:

I am a career coach; I help executives . . . build their digital brands.
I am a career branding strategist; I help career coaches . . . map out their processes.
I am a digital branding specialist; I help recruiters . . . build content marketing funnels.

So That

The final part of your personal brand statement is not for you; it is aimed directly at your audience. It's the benefit they receive from working with you. Whenever you are working on anything, there is a transformation you want to take place.

The transformation depends on what you want to be known for, who you help, and what you want them to understand or do. Whatever the transformation is, it's important to remember that the outcome is aimed at your audience, not you.

The "so that" portion of your personal branding statement acts to draw in your targeted audience. As they become more intrigued by what you do, it will lead to additional questions and the opportunity to further explain how you can help them. Pulling all the framework together looks something like this:

I am a career coach; I help executives build their digital brands . . . so they can be found in search and get recognized for their expertise.

I am a career branding strategist; I help career coaches map out their processes . . . so they can develop a cohesive marketing and branding strategy.

I am a digital branding specialist; I help recruiters build content marketing funnels . . . so they can collect and nurture more leads for their open positions.

Final Adjustments

It might take you awhile to put your statement together, but once you believe you have it, read it out loud to yourself. Do you think it accurately describes you and how you add value? Can you say it with confidence? Can you give examples of times when you've put your statement to work?

If you answered yes to these questions, congratulations. You've just created your personal brand statement! If you're not quite there yet, keep at it. Tweak it as often as you like. If you feel stuck, share your personal brand statement with a friend, coworker, or trusted advisor. Ask for their input. Keep refining it until you stop and say, "Yep, that's me!"

Final Thoughts on the Define Step

I know—it's a lot. The Define step is challenging because it involves so much learning and thinking about yourself. The good news is, though, by now you know and understand yourself better than you ever have before. You know what makes you tick, you know where you add the most value, and you know what it is you want to be known for.

Congratulations! Now the "fun" begins. For the rest of this book, you'll be focused on leveraging your brand online, and it all begins with the Integrate step.

The Define Step Checklist

- ☐ Take the Digital Brand Assessment
- ☐ Score: ______________

Step #1 - Self Awareness

- ☐ Complete the Introspection exercise
- ☐ Download Memo Mailer (Optional)
- ☐ Complete the Skills and Traits worksheet
- ☐ Complete the Values
- ☐ Send email to Trusted Advisors
- ☐ Complete Trusted Advisor worksheet
- ☐ Identify Assessments to take
- ☐ Complete Assessment worksheet

Step #2 - What do you want to be known for?

- ☐ Complete the Future You worksheet

Step #3 - Personal Brand Statement

- ☐ Complete the Personal Brand Statement worksheet

Part Four

The Integrate Step

"The line between online and offline is blurring." —Tim Kopp

Unlock the power of your brand by combining your offline and online activities.

Digital Brand Assessment Score: 26–50

Assessment takers with a score between twenty-six and fifty can usually be found in the Integrate step. I say *usually* because if your score is between twenty-six and thirty-five, it's possible that your unique name has placed you here while your digital brand may still be in the Define step.

Most people in the Integrate step are aware of personal and digital brands. You may have already started or are just beginning to build your brand and online presence. You may have a few social media or personal brand page accounts set up, but your use of them is sporadic at best.

More than likely, you have not yet considered using your accounts strategically in a way that works to your advantage. It's possible that Google is still in control of your online presence.

People who find themselves with a score in this range often think:

I want recruiters to find me online.
I want to build a comprehensive brand.
I am an expert in my field but do not communicate this enough.
I want to gain exposure online.
I am invisible online.

If one or more of these thoughts resonate with you, the good news is that the Integrate step will help you answer these questions. It's time to push Google aside and take charge of your digital brand.

Chapter 16

Invisibility

Matthew Capala is the founder of Alphametric, a company that specializes in helping companies increase their visibility and profitability through search engine optimization. During my interview with him on the *BRAND New You Show* podcast, we were having a great conversation about how developing a personal brand is a must in order to advance in one's career, when he said something that struck me hard and has become something I think about every day:

> "Invisibility is a fate worse than failure."

Worse than failure. I don't believe the ramifications of this statement have ever been truer for business professionals today. I do believe it will only amplify in the coming years.

We live in a world where 80 percent of consumers search online before they buy a product. It won't be long before that number approaches 100 percent. Yes, that number is for those "consumers" who search for products online. However, today when a recruiter or hiring manager is searching for someone to fill an open position, don't you think they search online as well?

Of course they do.

According to a survey by Jobvite, a company that makes software for recruiting, 92 percent of recruiters take to the online "streets" when searching for candidates.[6] The probability is very high that, right now,

---

6 Jobvite. (2015). The Jobvite Recruiter Nation Survey 2015. Retrieved from https://www.jobvite.com/wpcontent/uploads/2015/09/jobvite_recruiter_nation_2015.pdf.

as you read this sentence, there is a recruiter out there typing a potential candidate's name—maybe yours—into Google or LinkedIn to see what comes up.

If they like what they see, they might buy your "product" in the form of an email or phone call to you. On the hand, if you don't show up in search, you are as good as invisible to them and they are off to the next potential candidate.

Now before you get the bright idea that you can just create a few online profiles and show up in a search, think again. Showing up is important, but showing up in the manner in which you want to be found is more important.

Congruency Is the Key

I hear it all the time:

> "You have to be authentic."

> "Authenticity is the key to building your brand."

While I agree that being authentic is important, I also think it's expected. It's the same as breathing is to living. We all know breathing is a key factor for living, yet no one goes around saying, "You have to breathe in order to live."

I view authenticity in the same way.

So for the sake of argument and for the "authenticity" torchbearers out there, I'll stipulate that authenticity is important when building your personal brand. But when it comes to establishing your CareerKred online, it's not THE most important thing to consider. Being congruent is.

Most of us associate the word *congruent* with math, which is probably why we don't regularly include it in our vocabulary. Being congruent means to be matching—to be in harmony or in agreement with something. The *Urban Dictionary* says that congruency is when someone is consistent with their actions and personality, (they are) unique to themselves.

Being unique to yourself is the definition of Authenticity. I find it interesting that the same phrase is within the definition of *congruency* as well.

Authenticity and self-awareness are the cornerstones of the Define step. However, during the Integrate step, congruency becomes the cornerstone for integrating your brand online. It's the key to getting recognized for your expertise, growing your influence, and amplifying your CareerKred.

Congruency in Action

Think about the last time you Googled someone. What did you do when the results were returned? I'm betting that even before you clicked on the top result, you scanned the page in order to ensure that you had the right person. You wanted to see if everything was in alignment and the results matched your expectations.

As a career coach and podcaster conducting research on guests, I am always looking for congruency. Something as simple as having the same headshot image across all of your social media accounts is tremendously helpful in letting me know I have found the right person.

Recruiters and hiring managers are no different. Tim Saumier is the founder and CEO of Tyges, an executive recruiting agency. During our podcast conversation, Tim told me he does the exact same thing. In fact, he offered this advice when I asked him what candidates should do before they begin a job search:

> Before you start to look for a job, get your backyard in order. Take care of your online profile. Make sure that what you're saying on Facebook to your buddy from college isn't going to show up.

For those of you who may be a little skeptical about building an online presence, I asked Tim what he felt was more important today: a good resume or a good online presence. Here's what he had to say:

> I would tell you a good online presence (is more important) bar none. I can convince companies that I work with to talk to an individual without a resume. I can't convince them to do this if the candidate is on Facebook using foul language or inappropriate videos or whatever. I can't convince companies to talk to them then.

This is the power of congruency.

If a search result is perceived to be out of place or out of alignment with your expectations, you will immediately start to question the credibility of the person you just looked up.

When building your CareerKred, that's why it's important to take the time during the Integrate phase to plan before you execute. Proper planning and execution will ensure that when you turn up in a search, you will appear congruent and in alignment. There will be no red flags.

It's also why when I begin the Integrate step with my clients, the first thing we do is a digital audit.

Exercise 9—Digital Audit

For this exercise, I want you to put yourself in Tim Saumier's shoes. He's just come across your resume, pulled up Google, and typed your name in the search bar. Is Tim going to find a congruent digital brand?

Let's find out.

1. Sign out of your current browser, then open an incognito or private browsing window.
2. Google yourself. Use the name people will use when they search for you.
3. Capture all the search results using the worksheet in the *CareerKred Workbook* (http://careerkredbook.com/workbook).

With the results in front of you, answer the following questions.

- Do the results tell the story you want to be told?
- Are the results congruent?
- Would someone who does not know you get a good idea of who you are?
- Are you recognizable from someone who may share your name?
- Do the results represent what you want to be known for?

This exercise should serve to open your eyes to the importance of your online profile. Remember, if you want to be known for knowing something, you have to be that something everywhere. You have to be congruent. Especially online.

Without first defining your brand, what usually happens is that you'll unintentionally create the smattering of an online profile that will convey nothing of value to anyone who searches for you. You may appear in the search results, but it won't be in a manner that paints you as the expert you are—in which case you may as well be invisible.

That's why the DICE process starts with defining your brand.

Integrate Step 1

Chapter 17

Your Career Story

Complacency—it happens to all of us. When you've been working in the same industry, doing the same job for a period of time, two things happen.

First, you get to know your role very well. So well, in fact, that you often forget the "small stuff" you do on a daily basis. Second, you forget the technical skills you needed when you started out as well as many of the additional ones you've learned along the way.

The side effect of this is that you begin to look at your career as a series of bullet points instead of experiences. You forget everything you have to offer. That's why in this section you're going to take an in-depth dive into your career story.

You already know your personal brand tagline, but it's designed to be more of a conversation starter and a way to keep you focused in the areas where you add the most value. After you say it out loud, what do you say when you're asked the inevitable follow-up question about your experiences? This is where your career story comes into play.

Your career story, at a high level, is the combination of every position you've held in your career, the skills you've gained, and the experiences you've had. The challenge is not only remembering it all, but being able to tell your story in a relevant way.

Most career professionals rely on their resume to tell their story. This is a shame because a resume is nothing but a laundry list of jobs, skills, and accomplishments. A resume doesn't allow you to add commentary or share how you accomplished a specific goal.

So rather than rely on your resume alone, you need to create a career biography in order to tell your career story.

Exercise 10—Creating Your Career Biography

You will need the Your Career Biography worksheet from the *CareerKred Workbook* to complete this exercise. You can download the workbook at http://careerkredbook.com/workbook.

Next, grab your current resume; we'll use it as a guide to help us get started.

At the top of the worksheet, write your personal brand tagline. Now, take some time to complete the rest of the boxes on the sheet. List everything you can think of for each section—do not edit yourself.

After you've completed the worksheet, take a few minutes to draft a comprehensive career biography using everything on the sheet. Again, do not edit yourself; just write.

As you write, keep your audience in the back of your mind as you create your career biography. Make sure to address both the value you add and what you want to be known for.

Like the personal brand statement exercise, after you have an initial draft, start to revise and refine your career biography.

Once completed, the next step is to tailor your career biography into the four categories listed below.

- A LinkedIn summary—must be less than two thousand words
- A speaker bio—usually no longer than two paragraphs with up to three sentences in each
- A website bio—as many words as you like (it's your website, after all)
- Social media bios—depends on the platform, but a good rule of thumb is no more than 160 characters

Completing this exercise will not only provide you with a career story for different platforms, but it will go a long way toward helping you remain congruent online.

Integrate Step 2

Chapter 18

The Personal Website

By now it should be clear: We live in a digital-first world. Because of this, chances are great that your first interaction with a recruiter or hiring manager will be via your online presence. You will literally be making a first impression even while you sleep. That's why I recommend that every career professional have his or her own personal website.

Having a website is a great way to stand out from your competition. In fact, a survey commissioned by branded.me (now remote.com) and conducted by the about.me registry found that only 4 percent of professionals have a personal website.[7]

Having a website puts you at an immediate advantage, but if you're still hesitant, here are some other reasons websites are important.

- 93 percent of recruiters search for you online BEFORE you get a call.[8]
- 75 percent of Google searchers never look beyond page one.[9]
- 70–80 percent of users rely on organic search.[10]

---

7 Macario, Nick & Djukanovic, N. (2015) New landmark study shows link between personal websites and career success. Retrieved from http://ryanrhoten.com/what-is-branded-me/.

8 Jobvite. (2015). The Jobvite Recruiter Nation Survey 2015. Retrieved from https://www.jobvite.com/wp-content/uploads/2015/09/jobvite_recruiter_nation_2015.pdf.

9 Nair, S. (2016) Smart Hiring Techniques: A roadmap to hire digital marketers. Retrieved from http://www.business2community.com/seo/smart-hiring-techniques-road-map-hire-digital-marketers-01665343#3FTEKmghygWK6zLe.97.

10 Ibid.

A website gives you a platform from which you can tell your story and boost your CareerKred. Best of all, a website is something you control 100 percent. This is especially important in our digital-first age where people turn to Google for answers to everything.

Google

I think it's important at this point for you to fully understand what Google is and how it works. Don't worry; this will by no means be an in-depth review of Google's internal workings. Think of it instead as a high-level look at Google's role in the Integrate step.

You probably already know that Google is a search engine, but do you know what a search engine actually is? Google defines a *search engine* as "a program that searches for and identifies items in a database that correspond to keywords or characters specified by the user, used especially for finding particular sites on the Internet."

Without going into too much detail, Google maintains a directory of every site on the Internet. It "indexes," or groups together, websites of similar content for easy retrieval later. How does it know when sites have similar content? Because, among other things, Google looks at the keywords used within the content on the site.

Keywords

Did you know that keywords are what drives the web? A quick search for the term *keywords* on our friend Google defines them in the following manner: "A word or concept of great significance; an informative word used in an information retrieval system to indicate the content of a document."

Keywords are the informative words that search engines like Google use to identify content and other useful information. Anytime you type something into Google, you are typing in a keyword. Keywords can and usually do contain more than one word. Your name, for example, becomes a keyword once someone types it in the search bar and presses enter.

A big part of getting found online is making sure that your keywords—such as your name and any words associated with what you want to be known for—are displayed on the first page of results when people search for you.

Take a minute to think about the Google search you did on your name earlier. Consider all of the sites on the Internet, social media included, where your name appears. When someone types in your name, Google finds and groups all of the sites together where your name appears. This way, when someone searches for you, Google knows where to look and will quickly return those results.

For instance, when I search for my name, Google returns 91,400 results in .41 seconds. How many results does Google provide when you search for your name?

With keywords and Google in mind, there is no better way to get found and become recognized for your expertise then to have your name indexed on the Internet.

Starting Your Own Website

I get it—the thought of starting your own website is intimidating. I've heard this argument a lot. I was right there with you five years ago when I started my first website. I may have given you a different recommendation back then, but a lot has changed, and I'm here to tell you starting a website is a lot easier than it used be.

There are basically two ways for you to build a website. One way is to Do It Yourself (DIY) or, if you don't have the time or technical know-how, you can go the Done For You (DFY) route. Either way works—what's important is that you end up with a website.

Chapter 19

The DIY Website

Building a website yourself is both rewarding and at times frustrating. It's rewarding because when you are finished you can look at your work and say, "I did that." Additionally, you'll also be learning some new skills along the way. To help you get started building your own website, here are the DIY steps you need to take.

Step 1—Buy Your Domain

In order to have a website, you first need a domain. Think of a domain as your home address on the Internet. It's your place on the Web. It's where you will send people to learn more about you and how you add value to the world. Domains are inexpensive; they run about twelve dollars a year.

To build your digital brand, I recommend purchasing your name (first and last) as your domain—i.e., www.yourname.com. Even if you have no plans to build a website, you should still purchase your domain for no other reason than to prevent someone else from purchasing it.

Why your first and last name? Because if YOU don't own your domain someone else who shares your name could buy it. Once they own it, it's theirs, and they can do whatever they want with it, whether you like it or not. If you doubt this, check out http://tedcruz.com (as of January 2017).

Now, before you tell me you have a unique name and you don't have to worry, you should know that there are only *four* Ryan Rhotens in the entire world. When I decided to purchase ryanrhoten.com, guess what? One of the other Ryans already owned it.

Choosing your name as your domain will help you get found easier in searches, and you'll be able to "attach" your name to the keywords you want to be known for. When purchasing your name, make sure you choose the name people know you by, the name people will use when they search for you, or the name you use on your resume.

What do you do if your name is already taken? This does happen, especially if you have a common name, such as Michael Smith. If this is the case for you, try a variation of your first and last name such as ryanlrhoten.com, theryanrhoten.com, ryanrhotenhq.com.

Sabrina Clark, marketing manager at brandyourself.com, recommends in these cases that you use a qualifier in your domain, such as writer, product manager, or real estate. In this case your domain would look like this: ryanrhotenwriter.com, ryanrhotenproductmanager.com, or ryanrhotenrealestate.com.

While I agree that this method gets your name in the domain, I would caution you to make sure that you're happy with whatever qualifier you select and that it aligns with what you want to be known for. Two years down the road, if you decide to not be a product manager anymore, for example, you're still stuck with the ryanrhotenproductmanager.com domain.

As a first choice, always try to buy the .com extension. It's popular and people naturally remember it. If the .com version of your domain is already taken, I recommend using a .me extension. In my case, it would be ryanrhoten.me.

You can purchase your domain from a number of accredited registrars. A few of the most popular are Namecheap, Go Daddy, Host Gator, and Bluehost.

PRO TIP: If you are a parent (or grandparent) consider buying your children's or grandchildren's names as well. This will prevent someone else with the same name from purchasing it.

Regardless of which provider you choose, once your payment has been processed, you are now the proud owner of an Internet address. This is where you'll send people to share your message and start building your CareerKred.

Congrats! You are now one step closer to having a website you can call your own. But (there's always a *but*, isn't there?) owning your domain is like knowing the address for the plot of land where you will live. In order to actually live there, however, you will need to purchase the land, and this is where hosting comes into play.

Step 2—Hosting Your Website

In order to have a website, in addition to your Internet (street) address, you'll also need access to the land. Hosting buys the land you'll build your house on. In other words, hosting secures space for your website on a server.

Your hosting account is where all of the files for your website will be stored and assigned to the Internet. Fortunately, the same companies that sell you your domain will also provide you with hosting. I recommend buying your domain and your hosting from the same company. It just makes things easier.

Hosting costs vary from provider to provider, but you should never pay more than $100 a year when starting out. In order to help keeps your costs down, I recommend using Bluehost. The interesting thing about Bluehost is that they don't sell individual domains. They sell hosting and then give you the domain name for free. Bluehost hosting plans starting as low as $3.95 a month, which translates to less than $50 a year.

Once you've purchased your domain and hosting, you own both the land and the address. Think of your purchase as a property tax for your house. As long as you pay the tax, you "own" the real estate. It might surprise you, but at this point you don't have a website quite yet. What you have is the domain (address) and the hosting (reserved space for your files on a server).

Now, you need to start construction on your house, starting with its foundation. This means you need a content management system (CMS for short).

Step 3—Content Management System

A content management system (CMS) is a computer application that allows you to publish, edit, and modify content from a central interface on the Web. CMS applications help you manage workflow in such a simplified way that even a total newbie can create a great looking website.

When it comes to choosing a CMS, you have many options. Personally, I'm a huge fan of WordPress. WordPress is installed on nearly 75 million websites, which accounts for roughly 19 percent of all the sites on the Web. Popular sites like CNN, TechCrunch, eBay, Best Buy, and Fortune all use WordPress.

To use WordPress, you'll need to install it on your server, and lucky for us, this can be done with the click of a mouse. I realize this part can be daunting, so I created a video at https://ryanrhoten.com/blogsetup to walk you through the steps required to install WordPress.

With WordPress installed, you officially have a home on the Internet.

Chapter 20

The DFY Website

If the notion of building a site yourself scares you, then a Done For You site might be the way to go. This option will cost you a little more money, but it may also save you a lot of time and hassle.

There is another catch to this method in addition to the cost. You will still need to learn how to use the CMS in order to be able to make updates and publish blog posts. More on that a little later.

There are many choices when it comes to DFY websites. Some of the more popular ones include Squarespace, Wix, Weebly, Go Daddy, WordPress.com, and the new Google Sites platform. All of these websites will help you get up and running with very little technical knowledge required on your part.

While these platforms will do the job, there is a new one I've run across that fits in between them: Build Your Digital Brand. Founded by Jennifer Bonoff, Build Your Digital Brand is a personal branding and digital marketing service designed to help individuals stand out by building custom-branded websites designed to attract opportunities for its clients.

Jennifer is co-chair of the Department of Business Studies and Economics, Marketing Area coordinator, and instructor of Marketing at both the undergraduate and graduate levels at a local university. In her role, she recognized the need for business professionals to build their digital brands, so she decided to start a company to help them do it.

What I like about Build Your Digital Brand as a solution for you is the service and the price. For $199 plus $10 or $25 a month (depending on the package you choose), you can have a professional website created for you. Included in the price is access to customer service, a digital brand training course, and monthly hosting and maintenance.

If you're interested in learning more about this solution, check out http://buildyourdigitalbrand.com. As a bonus, if you enter the coupon code BYDBRR at checkout, you'll receive a $10 discount on your package.

Chapter 21

Pages on Your Website

Regardless of which option you choose, DIY or DFY, the next thing you'll need to know is what pages you should include and what is appropriate and not appropriate to put on your personal website. These are two very different questions. We'll cover what to put on your site in the Create step.

As far as building your website goes, in addition to the home page, I suggest having the following pages on your website: a Career page, a Blog page, an About page, and a Contact page. Note: These pages can change depending on your goals.

Career Page

More than a LinkedIn profile and well beyond a typical resume, a career page is the place where you expand on your past and current roles and experiences. It provides you with a place to tell the story of HOW you accomplished the achievements you list on your resume.

Your personal website should not be a bullet point list of your accomplishments—your resume already does this. Instead, use your website to expand on your accomplishments in a way you can't on your resume.

For example, explain how you accomplished a particular result despite only having a staff of two for a project that requires ten people. Telling your story in this manner allows would-be employers to get a feel for you as an individual, and more importantly, it provides them with a glimpse into how you would fit into their culture.

Blog Page

Let me start by saying something that may seem controversial. Your personal website should not be used to share pictures of your animals, your food, or your thoughts on politics. Especially not politics—unless, of course, your career goal is to stay exactly where you are right now and never get promoted, or you want to move into the political arena.

Instead, you need to post brief, well-thought-out posts on your area of expertise. In today's job market, companies are looking for original thinkers, risk-takers, people who go beyond just talking about the same old stuff. A thoughtful blog post can help a company get a feel for who you are and how you would potentially fit with its culture.

If you're struggling with ideas about what to post, think about the important topics in your industry. Have you recently read an interesting article on a specific topic in your industry and disagreed with it? If so, write about why you disagreed with the author's stance and offer a different perspective. Do you have a new idea or a best practice about your field? Write a blog post about it.

During your trip to the Himalayas, did you uncover a unique take on a topic that can be applied to your industry? If so, write about it. The point of the Blog page is to help the audience get to know and (hopefully) like you. If your blog posts resonate with them, you might just get a phone call. Don't worry, we'll cover more on blog posts in the Create step.

About Page

It should go without saying but you need an About page on your website—but maybe not for the reason you think. Your About page is not a place for you to tell the world about your dog, your cat, or any other domesticated animal you happen to own. It's also not the place to discuss your most recent vacation.

Instead, your About page should convey an understanding of the issues and challenges your audience (clients) face and what you do to help resolve them. Remember the website bio you created at the beginning of the Integrate step? This is where it goes.

Now, that's not to say you can't have fun with your About page. In fact, the About page is where I recommend you let your personality show. Just remember to do it in a way that links back to your career story and what you want to become known for.

Contact Page

A Contact page is another must. How else will people reach out to you? You'll also need to list an email address on this page. However, if your email is bigkitten48, John117, IhateMyJob, or something else nonprofessional, it's time to get a new email address. That email address was funny when you created it ten years ago, but if you're using your site to further your career goals, it's time to say sayonara.

And while you're at it, drop the Hotmail, AOL, EarthLink, and other outdated email extensions you may have. Using them conveys you're as outdated as the email provider.

Do include a phone number on your contact page. Why? Because there are still people out there who like to speak with candidates. Recruiters fall into this description and might be one of the last professions that still relies on a phone for communication.

Now, before you wig out about putting your phone number online, there is another way. You can sign up for a free Google Voice account at http://google.com/voice. This allows you to provide a phone number for people to contact you that is not your personal phone.

This also provides you with a phone number to put on your LinkedIn page as well. What? You haven't put any contact information on your LinkedIn page yet?

Finally, you need to include links to all your social media profiles. This makes it very easy for people to find out more about you; it's a convenience thing. They will eventually find all of your social profiles anyway, so why not link them to where they are? This is especially important if you share a name with someone else.

I've just given you a lot of information about getting your website set-up, but there is one point that bears repeating. Having a personal website is a great way to stand out from competition and boost your CareerKred in your field of choice.

Exercise 11—Set Up Your Website

This exercise should come as no surprise: The first step to becoming visible in a digital-first world is having your own address online. Here is a summary of the high-level steps you'll need to take to get your DIY website started:

- **Buy your domain.**
- **Host your domain**—I recommend using Bluehost for hosting and purchasing your domain. Investing in both with the same company will save you steps later.
- **Install a content management system (CMS)**—I recommend WordPress.
- **Start blogging**—We'll discuss blogging in detail during the Create step.

I know setting up your website can be intimidating, but it's critical to building your brand online. If you get hung up, stuck, or don't think you have the technical expertise, I do have a couple of free online resources to help you.

The first resource can be found at http://RyanRhoten.com/blogsetup. This five minute video will walk you step-by-step through the process of purchasing your domain and hosting, installing WordPress, and even making your very first post.

The second resource can be found at http://careerbranding.academy. This course is specifically designed to get you up and running with WordPress. The course contains thirteen videos that walk you through how to use the various menus on your WordPress dashboard.

If DFY is your thing, don't forget to check out Build Your Digital Brand. Their pricing is very competitive, and you'll get excellent results. If you use the coupon code BYDBRR at checkout, you'll receive a $10 discount on your package.

Integrate Step 3

Chapter 22

Personal Brand Landing Pages

Creating a website is the most critical step to integrating your brand online. This is also the step where I get the most pushback from my clients who are reluctant to build a website. They often ask, "Why would I start a website when I can set up an account on a personal brand landing page for free?" It's a fair question, so let's take a deeper look.

You can probably guess already that I am not a big fan of using personal brand landing pages as the main place to build your brand online. But they are important strategically, so I want to take a minute to give you my definition for personal brand landing pages and explain how you can use them effectively as a part of your overall Integration strategy.

First, the definition: A personal brand landing page is a single profile page on the Web designed to attract attention and get straight to the point about who you are and what you do. I like to think of personal brand landing pages as billboards on the Internet highway.

Like billboards, their job is to convey to the reader information about you quickly. Think of the last billboard you saw while driving. What message did it convey? Why did it capture your attention?

The initial purpose of both the billboard and your personal brand landing page is to capture attention.

The second purpose of the billboard—and arguably the most important—is that it tells you where to go to learn more. A billboard on a real highway will tell you how many miles you have left to go and what exit to take to get there. Your personal brand landing page, when used strategically, will do the same.

Essentially landing pages act as a lead generation tool to send your potential audience somewhere else. That somewhere else might be your website, your music page, or wherever else you want to send them.

Use Your Personal Brand Landing Page Strategically

Personal brand landing pages are usually free and quick to set up. They can be used as a way to quickly provide an Internet superhighway traveler with information about you and the problems you help solve, which means they have the ability to drive visitors to your site.

But most people don't realize the real secret behind personal brand landing pages: backlinks. Backlinks serve as signals to Google. The more backlinks you have to your website, the more Google will recognize it as important.

We use personal brand landing pages during the Integrate step to pull together all of your social profiles in one place and, most importantly, provide you with a backlink to your site.

Remember earlier when we discussed how Google groups together like content by keywords? Your personal brand landing page will not only show a link back to your site (a backlink), but it will also contain a critical keyword on the page (your name).

Since your page includes links to your other profiles as well, it actually helps Google understand that all of your profiles are linked. Pretty slick, eh?

Take a minute here and think about the Internet. Consider all of the different pages and profiles you can create. Each page or profile is separate and unique. The only thing that exists on each of those pages that may be common is your name.

But Google won't necessarily know that your name on all of those separate pages is you. What if you share your name with someone else, as I mentioned earlier? Using your personal brand landing page to link all or most of these separate pages together helps Google know that you are you.

Personal Brand Landing Page or Website?

There are a multitude of personal brand landing pages you could use. I predict that, as we continue to realize the power of the Web for our brands and our careers, even more will pop up in the future. Out of the multitudes that currently exist at the time of writing this book, I recommend using About.me for building your brand.

While I recommend using About.me, I do so only in the context mentioned above. Personal brand landing pages are meant to be used as billboards in your strategy, not your main address on the Web. You don't own them, and relying on them as the sole method to integrate your brand online is dangerous because if the business behind the landing page folds, so does your page. You lose everything.

If you think back to my earlier analogy, a website is a place where you can build your brand on land you have purchased. As long as you continue to pay your annual fee (your property tax), you will always have access to your site.

Building your brand on personal brand landing pages, on the other hand, is like building on rented land. If the landlord comes to you one day and says he's sold the property or gone bankrupt, guess what happens to your personal brand landing page? Your page could very easily vanish overnight. If you think this is an extreme example, remember that technology is constantly changing, both in advancement and popularity.

What if you had chosen MySpace as the place to build your brand back in the day? This is why I recommend using personal brand landing pages as tools to capture attention, drive people to your website, and capture backlinks.

If used in this manner, a personal brand landing page can serve as a useful tool when building your brand online. With this in mind, let's explore one popular personal brand landing page option, About.me.

About.me

About.me was founded in 2009 and officially launched in 2010. This is how About.me defines itself on its About page:

> *We believe that you should own your own identity. That your identity should be both projected and protected. It should encompass the different*

facets of your life. It should be portable and universally accessible. And most importantly, it should be easy to create and manage.

That's a lot of words to say that you can easily create and manage a page on the Internet. About.me is free to join, requiring only your name and email address to get started.

Once you sign up you get immediate access to begin creating your homepage. It's a very simple, step-by-step process. There is absolutely zero coding knowledge required on your part. It's so simple that you can have a page up in as little as five minutes.

You can customize the page to your heart's content within the parameters of the software. Everything from colors, fonts, and background images to links and contact info can all be customized. This allows you to keep your branding consistent across platforms.

Some tips to keep in mind as you build your page are to include links to both your social media accounts and your website. Make sure you use consistent fonts and colors, as this will help people identify you. Speaking of which, make sure you include a picture of yourself. A good one, not a selfie (more on that later).

About.me also offers a paid option. For $80 a year, you can buy your domain and use their hosting service. If you use the free account, which is what I do, your domain will reside at about.me/your-name. Buying your domain through them will allow you to use yourname.me as your domain, which removes their branding.

Exercise 12—Personal Brand Landing Pages

In this exercise you will take the time to set up your personal brand landing page on About.me.

About.me

To get started with About.me, head to the About.me website and sign up using select social media accounts or an email address. Clicking any of the buttons will take you through the sign-up process.

When selecting your page name, make sure you use the same name you selected as your domain name when you set up your website. Remember, congruency is key.

Just follow the setup wizard to get your profile up and running.

Integrate Step 4

Chapter 23

Social Media

One of the most common reservations I hear from people about building their brand online is that they don't want to "put themselves out there" on the Internet. Instead, they want to remain anonymous.

In other words, they want to be invisible. We've already discussed the negative ramifications of remaining invisible in today's job market earlier in the book, so here I'll just point out that ironically, usually these people already have some sort of social media account.

If you have an account on social media, you are already "out there." Instead of eschewing social media, embrace it and use it for good. After all, it's not going anywhere.

I like to compare Social media to the Force in *Star Wars*. It can be powerful, and it can used for good or evil. It can help build your brand, but it can also destroy your brand in an instant.

In his book, *A World Gone Social*, Mark Babbitt says there are essentially two types of people on social media today: Relentless Givers and Askholes. Can you guess on which side of the Force each one resides?

Askholes

More often than not, when speaking with people who do not want to put themselves out there, I find that at some point in their social journey, they ran into an Askhole. See if you can relate.

An Askhole is someone who asks for something the first time they send you a tweet or message you on Facebook. They might be asking you to buy something, download something, or give them something—usually your time.

Askholes, Mark told me, don't take the time to shake your hand digitally and try to build a relationship. Instead they throw out the ask on the first communication. I think you'd agree this is unacceptable.

Askholes are the ones who fill up your Twitter feeds with messages of me, me, me. Unfortunately for us, social media enables these behaviors because, as Mark told me, if we don't have any filters in our non-digital lives, we're probably not going to have any filters when we are hitting the keyboard either.

Relentless Givers

On the flip side of Askholes are the Relentless Givers. Relentless Givers give of themselves and serve others while at the same time championing their own brands. They are very giving and honestly want to help others succeed as they move their own mission forward. Their mindset is: Together we all grow.

This is an important distinction to help understand the value of social media when building your brand. This Relentless Giver mindset tells us it's okay to serve our own purpose and move our own missions forward, but at the same time, why not share what you know with others?

Why not be a knowledge database, a connector for others with common thoughts, common principles, and common goals? The simple truth is that, if we give of ourselves, we have the ability to improve the lives of everybody around us.

Like an athlete on the field of play, the Relentless Giver's primary goal is to make the entire team better, not just one person. According to Mark, Relentless Givers work collectively to make us all better so when it comes time to compete, all of us are going to be more ready to step up.

I can think of no better example of a Relentless Giver than Jared Easley. Jared is a coauthor of the book *Stop Chasing Influencers* and a cofounder of the world's largest podcasting conference, Podcast

Movement. Jared first introduced me to the power of relentless giving through his podcast, and he continues to amaze me with his generosity today.

He is constantly looking for ways he can help his network grow. Whether through a tweet or an email, he uses his platform to connect as many people as he can. You can hear it in his podcast, *Starve the Doubts*, as well as in every conversation he has. If you've not heard of Jared, I urge you to listen to his podcast.

Jared truly believes that by constantly helping others achieve their goals, every one of the people you've helped along the way will be more inclined to help you when you need it. Being a Relentless Giver builds up good networking karma, and that's just a no-brainer in today's social world. Imagine if we all followed Jared's lead?

Why You Need to Be Social Today

It used to be enough just to have a social media account. Those days have changed. Merely having an account today is like attending a networking event only to stand in the corner and not talk to anyone. Today, if you want to stand out and build your CareerKred, you have to work the digital room.

Having a LinkedIn profile, for example, doesn't guarantee that a recruiter is going to find you. How many of you reading this right now are frustrated because you don't get enough attention from recruiters? I hear this frustration expressed every week by my clients. You have this terrific background of skills and experiences, yet you get virtually no contacts from recruiters.

The reason for is this simple: Recruiters and hiring managers are moving beyond assessing for skills and experiences. What they are really searching for today are candidates that will fit in with the company. Having the right skills and experiences no longer set you apart; they have become the expectation, the norm.

Recruiters today want to see more than a list of bullet points; instead, they want to understand your thought process and, most importantly, *how* you achieved your list of accomplishments. You cannot tell anyone how you achieved anything using bullet points alone (despite what PowerPoint would have you believe). According to Don Orlando, career coach and LinkedIn expert:

> Hiring managers today go where the folks they are looking for hang out virtually. When they get there, they are looking for your contributions, specifically the *quality* of your contributions. When they find someone whose quality of contribution is high, that's when they will take the time to Google you or to reach out.

Don's comment aligns perfectly with the Relentless Giver concept. If you are "out there" contributing in a meaningful way, genuinely trying to help others, the side effect will be that you'll get noticed. You will stand out from the crowd.

Zig Ziglar once said, "You will get all you want in life if you help enough other people get what they want." This is the Relentless Giver mantra, and this is what makes you stand out today. Bullet points and PowerPoints don't cut it anymore.

If you want to get noticed, strive to become a Relentless Giver. Decide to become social. In my opinion this is what the entire premise of social media rests on. As you help others get what they want, your CareerKred will rise, and you will be recognized for your expertise.

How to Choose?

My hope is that by now you understand that social media is a benefit to you and your career—assuming, of course, you stay with the good side of the Force and become a Relentless Giver.

If I've done my part correctly, at this point you're probably asking yourself, "Which social media platform should I be on?" Otherwise, please go back to the start of this section and reread it.

When people ask me this question, my response is always the same: Where does your audience hang out? Most people can't answer this question at this stage, which is why I recommend two platforms to get started: LinkedIn and Twitter. They offer a unique one-two punch for business professionals.

Chapter 24

LinkedIn

LinkedIn was founded in late 2002 and launched to the public in May 2003. Since then it has become the world's largest social network for professionals. At the time of this writing, there are over 400 million users.

With that many users you would think LinkedIn would be the social network of choice for business professionals. Unfortunately, this doesn't seem to be the case, and the reason is simple. LinkedIn is confusing to a lot of people, and frankly, this is a "label" that has been rightfully earned over the years for a couple of reasons.

First, people do not know what LinkedIn really is. Let me clarify it for you: LinkedIn is a networking tool. It is NOT Facebook. It is NOT an online resume.

LinkedIn is designed to help individuals, recruiters, and hiring managers find and make connections. As a registered user, you can establish and document your own professional network of people you know, like, and trust professionally.

This notion of LinkedIn as a networking tool is lost on many people, especially those who believe LinkedIn is an online resume. Can you put your experiences on LinkedIn? Yes. Can you add all your past positions to LinkedIn? Of course you can.

But this is not the point of LinkedIn. When used as a networking tool, LinkedIn allows you to connect with like-minded people inside and outside your industry. It's a tool to grow your network.

However, many people miss this point, treating LinkedIn as a virtual resume and then wondering why they are rarely contacted by recruiters and hiring managers. Rather than using their LinkedIn profile as a place to express their brand and demonstrate their unique promise of value, they "set it and forget it."

According to Don Orlando, it's easy for him to spot such a profile because it looks "exactly like an obituary."

The second reason people are confused about LinkedIn is that they don't realize that, like Google, LinkedIn is a search engine. Unlike Google, which searches the entire World Wide Web, LinkedIn uses its search engine to search within its 400 million members.

You may recall from our earlier discussion on Google that search engines rely on keywords to categorize and return results. If your profile reads like an obituary, it most likely contains very little or no keywords, or it contains the wrong keywords for the type of position you are seeking. Perhaps this is the reason why your profile does not get very many views.

Since many users do not understand LinkedIn, they miss out on one of the main benefits of using the platform: positioning themselves as experts in their field.

Positioning Yourself on LinkedIn

During my podcast interview with Kylie Chown and Jane Anderson, we talked about their book, *Connect: Leverage your LinkedIn Profile for Business Growth and Lead Generation*. Kylie pointed out that "the real key to your LinkedIn success is having a quality profile."

Jane expanded on this idea by adding, "people are making judgments about you that you don't even realize because of your LinkedIn profile." These judgments are directly related to how you use the platform. This gets back to our earlier discussion regarding perception in today's digital age. If you don't create the perception of yourself that you want others to have, they will create their own perception, which could be contrary to your goals.

Your profile is key to positioning yourself as an expert on LinkedIn and your goals are key to your positioning. Yes, you need to have goals for your LinkedIn profile.

Like anything else, Jane tells us that with LinkedIn, "You need to set goals for your profile specifically stating what do you want to do in the next twelve to eighteen months." Your LinkedIn profile should be about your future, not your past. If it focuses on your past, it will read like an obituary.

With this in mind, here are the ten sections of your LinkedIn profile you need to review and update in order to position yourself as an expert in your niche.

Your Headline (Title)

Everything starts with your headline. Jane Anderson stated during our discussion that we have roughly four seconds to capture someone's attention when they land on our profile. *Four seconds.* This can be a challenge when your headline is limited to 120 characters.

Just so we're clear, your professional headline is located directly below your name on your profile. By default, your headline will reflect your latest job title. This is how you can quickly tell whether or not the person has put any time into their profile or not. Nine times out ten, a job title headline translates into an obituary-like profile.

The headline is designed for two purposes. First, it should clearly explain who you are and how you add value—in other words, who you help or what problems you solve. This is where your career biography serves as a great starting point to narrow down your unique promise of value.

Second, your headline should serve as the first place to use the keywords you identified earlier. You should have two to three keywords in your professional headline, and they should speak directly to your positioning.

Your Profile Image

Right next to your headline is a place for you to upload an image of yourself. This is your digital-first impression. If you have not uploaded an image of yourself to LinkedIn, stop reading this book and do it now.

Don't just upload any image, though. Selfies are an absolute no-no on LinkedIn. You need an image that aligns with your brand and lets people know you are approachable. In my opinion, it must be a professional headshot.

I know some will disagree with this, but I would rather see an image of just your head and face filling up the entire 500 X 500 pixels than see a full body image of you in the same space. A full body image is at best very difficult to view.

In addition to a professional image that fills up the space, please make sure the image is recent. If I ever meet you in person, I want to be certain that it really is you because I've seen your profile image. That's the person I will be looking for.

Don't use an image of you from twenty years ago either. That may be fine for Facebook, but it doesn't work on LinkedIn.

Your Vanity URL

This might be the most overlooked feature on your LinkedIn profile. It's also the place I look to judge the depth of knowledge someone has about the platform. Your URL is the link you can provide to others so they can go directly to your profile rather than search for it. It is located directly below the profile box.

The majority of people who come to me looking for LinkedIn help have not updated their URL. It still looks something like this: https://www.linkedin.com/in/john-doe-58199216. Notice the numbers at the end? Remember, LinkedIn is a search engine. The easier you make it for the search engine to index your name, the better the chances you have of showing up in search.

What you need to do is turn the default URL into a vanity URL by getting rid of the numbers and making it more personal, like this: https://www.linkedin.com/in/ryanrhoten.

You can quickly update your URL by clicking the gear icon beside your current URL. Then, on the next page, in the top right box labeled Your Public Profile URL, click the edit icon and delete the numbers. Hint: You can also put a keyword here behind your name. For example, mine could be "ryanrhotencareercoach." Using a keyword in this location will not only help you show up in search results for your name, but for your keyword as well.

Your Connections

This should be obvious by now, but since LinkedIn is a networking tool, it makes sense that your connection count shows that you understand this. After all, this is a reflection of your network.

You should begin building your connections strategically versus just reaching out to anyone. Now that you have defined your brand, search for like-minded and influential people within your industry. This is how you begin to grow your audience and target network.

We'll talk more about how to use LinkedIn strategically later, but for now go ahead and start reaching out to people. Introduce yourself and ask how you can help. By the way, once you get above five hundred connections, LinkedIn no longer displays an exact number.

Your Summary

In normal circumstances, the summary is the hardest part of your LinkedIn profile to complete. For you, however, since you've completed all of the exercises up to this point, you can just copy and paste your shortened biography.

Remember, the summary section is limited to two thousand characters, and it should be a summary of your value. This is your brand statement. This is where you tell your audience the problems you solve and the context in which you solve them.

Michelle Robins, founder of Brand Your Career, provided a great tip regarding the LinkedIn summary I had not heard before. The first hundred characters in your summary show up below your name in the results from LinkedIn's recruiting tool. So as you build your summary, consider putting some contact information in those first one hundred characters. This is one place where I list my phone number.

Posts

Posts are LinkedIn's answer to the blog. Did you know that only about 1 percent of LinkedIn users publish content on the platform? If your goal is to differentiate yourself and stand out from your competition, publishing a post is a quick way for you to stand out.

Using the post feature in LinkedIn serves the same purpose as it does on your website, but the posts on LinkedIn have the potential to be distributed to a wider audience. I think posting on LinkedIn is a good thing because it allows you to share your insights with the world. In this way, you are demonstrating your expertise to others, and this will be noticed by recruiters and hiring managers.

Updates

Sharing articles via the Update feature that may be of interest to your audience is a great way to connect with them. Updates fall under content curation, which we'll discuss in detail in the Create step, but more importantly this can help establish you as a Relentless Giver.

Use your updates to share relevant content, and remember, this not Facebook. Professionally speaking, no one cares if your dog looks cute in a sweater.

Experience

Remember that the Experience section is not meant to be your resume. The Experience section is actually a search engine-optimized space in your LinkedIn profile. Think keywords.

Equally important is to remember that this section should be used to position yourself as an expert problem solver. Don Orlando summed this up best when he told me, "Everybody who has any sort of job worthy of being called a job is hired as a problem solver."

Use the experience section to highlight the problems you solve, how you solved them, and what the results were. This allows you to add context to your experiences, which will help viewers understand how you would fit within their organization's culture.

Another great feature in the Experience section is the ability to add media to each experience you list. Adding links to websites and articles you've written or have been featured in is a great way to showcase your expertise and make your profile "pop."

Don't underestimate the value adding media provides to your overall profile. It's a great way for you to demonstrate your expertise and show others the value you provide. Career Coach Marc Miller, founder of CareerPivot (one of the top one hundred career blogs according to *Forbes*), poses this question: "How do I know that you know your stuff?" Utilizing media within your experience section is a great place to start.

Groups

Yes, it is true that a lot of groups on LinkedIn suck, but many more don't. Like Twitter, which we'll discuss next, the Groups feature in

LinkedIn allows you to participate in the conversation about your industry. It's a great way to demonstrate your expertise.

Remember Don Orlando's earlier statement about hiring managers going where people hang out digitally. This is where you go to hang out on LinkedIn. Get involved in groups related to your field of expertise. Post content, answer questions, engage, and start building your reputation as a Relentless Giver.

Recommendations

Recommendations are another underutilized tool within your LinkedIn profile—which is unfortunate because recommendations can be very powerful. Jane Anderson explains the reason they are so powerful: "The person who wrote it is prepared to have their name associated with some commentary about you. This provides incredibly strong social proof."

Like or not, we live in a testimonial economy where we view recommendations as social proof. It's no longer enough for you to tell people how great you are; besides, no one likes to brag. It's way better when others do it for you.

Think about the last time you made a purchase on Amazon. Did you read the reviews? Most likely your answer is yes. Recommendations on your LinkedIn profile are becoming as important in today's economy as the testimonials you read on Amazon.

If you already have a few recommendations, you've got a head start over most users. If you don't have any, make a list of five to ten connections within your network you believe would recommend you and reach out to them. Offer to exchange recommendations you can both use on your profiles.

If reaching out "cold" bothers you, then try this approach instead. Identify people you would recommend to others, and write a recommendation for them. They will feel compelled to reciprocate.

Using LinkedIn for Integrating Your Brand

LinkedIn is one of the best ways for professionals today to quickly start integrating their brand online. As a bonus, Google seems to love the platform, evidenced by how high your LinkedIn profile can show up in search results.

For this reason, I encourage you to take your time and put together a complete LinkedIn profile. Complete all of the sections with as much information and stories as you can. Use the career biography you developed earlier, and expand on it in each section.

I am often asked about the premium version of LinkedIn. Full disclosure, I use the premium version. When I'm asked, I always follow the question up with another one: "What are your goals?"

Features of LinkedIn premium include the ability to send more InMails (messages to other LinkedIn members), you become a "featured applicant," and you can see who viewed your profile for the past ninety days. There are a few other features, but in my opinion these are the advantages over the basic plan.

If you're just getting started, stick with the basic plan. Use it until you know it inside and out. If you can't quite articulate your career goals, stick with the basic plan. No need to pay for something if you can't explain how it helps you achieve your goals.

If you took the digital brand assessment and your score was within the range of the Engage step, then you might want to consider the premium plan. As with anything else, there is a right time and a wrong time to use LinkedIn premium. My advice is to start slow; read that as stay with the basic plan. As you begin to see how your goals might be reached faster with the premium plan, then it's time to consider upgrading.

We'll discuss LinkedIn more in the Engage section, but now I want to introduce you to what I feel is the game-changing social media tool for all business professionals. This is especially true when used in conjunction with LinkedIn. I'm talking about Twitter.

Chapter 25

Twitter

For many, Twitter is a lot like LinkedIn—i.e., it's confusing. But as with LinkedIn, once you discover the real purpose and power behind Twitter, it is an amazing tool for you to boost your online reputation and enable you to be recognized for your expertise.

Madalyn Sklar from madalynsklar.com, a Twitter expert and founder of the Twitter Smarter and the Twitter Chat Playbook online courses, thinks one of the reasons people find Twitter so confusing is that "a lot of people are still in that mindset of 'that's the site you go to when you want to post pictures of what you had for breakfast.' No, that's not what we use it for."

Twitter launched in 2006 and has since grown to a network of over 310 million active users. At its core, rather than a platform for posting breakfast pictures, Twitter is a conversation-based, microblogging platform.

It's considered a microblog because users must get their message out using no more than 140 characters. Talk about the ultimate form of brevity. But Twitter is also so much more. It's a tool you can use to connect with other individuals and form relationships with them. It's a great tool to expand your network, demonstrate your expertise, and boost your Career-Kred. But that's not how most people see it when they first log on.

The Online Cocktail Party

David Fisher, from davidjpfisher.com and founder of Rock Start Consulting, likens Twitter to a "three hundred million-person networking cocktail reception." No wonder it can be overwhelming to new users!

It helps if you think of Twitter as an online cocktail party. This analogy is something I've heard over and over by my guests on the *BRAND New You Show* podcast. I think it's a great way to describe the platform and help you get past the confusion.

Imagine, if you will, Twitter as a bar. When you walk into the bar—-i.e., log onto your Twitter account—you look around and see lots of activity: people talking, music playing, servers taking drink orders. There's even the occasional "loud talker" that adds virtually no value but captures your attention, if only for a brief moment.

It's loud and it's confusing. Can you picture yourself at the entrance to your favorite bar? If so, what are doing as you stand there? Unless you are the first one to arrive, you are most likely looking for "your people." Once you find them, you cut through the crowd and take a seat.

Have you ever noticed how, once you find and join "your people" in the bar, all the loudness and confusion seems to fade into the background? There are even times when you don't hear the music playing or even notice the loud talker anymore. Why? Because you have become focused on the conversation you are having at your table. You're enjoying exchanging stories and sharing viewpoints. It's not quiet because everyone else has left; it's quiet because your focus has changed.

Now put yourself back at the entrance to the bar. Take a minute to observe what is actually happening. When you look at the bar (your Twitter feed), what you actually see is a lot of smaller groups of people speaking with "their people" in the bar.

Collectively, all of the smaller groups are contributing to the "loudness" of the platform. This is what you experience with Twitter initially, and that's why it can take some getting used to.

Katrina Collier, founder of thesearchologist.com, a social media recruitment training company, agrees. But she also knows from experience that if you take the time to learn the platform, "it's so worth getting your head around."

So the next time you open up your Twitter app or log in online, think of it as a big cocktail party, with lots of smaller conversations happening about all kinds of different topics and areas of interest.

Now that you grasp the concept behind Twitter, in order for you to really make use of the platform, you need to find your people.

Networking on Twitter

Connecting with other like-minded people and growing your network beyond just a collection of connections is the magic behind Twitter. It's what most people miss as they stand at the entrance to the bar and see the endless stream of tweets in their feed.

But as Madalyn reminds us, like a "cocktail party, it's common to go and introduce yourself to somebody on Twitter. It's a great place to connect." As it relates to integrating your brand online, Twitter may be the best place for you to make some great connections that can help you with your career.

Hannah Morgan, career coach and founder of the award-winning blog careersherpa.net, explained it to me this way: "Most people who are on Twitter are really open to networking. I don't think they would be on Twitter if they weren't open to networking. It's probably one of the more open, friendly places to meet people."

Like Hannah, I have had similar experiences. I use Twitter to connect, to share, and to establish relationships with people in the career space. It's because Twitter is such an open and receptive community that it has become the tool of choice for many career professionals, especially job seekers.

In conjunction with LinkedIn, Hannah suggests using Twitter as the tool to "go find people who work at the companies you want to work for and stalk them. Learn what they're about, learn what's important to them, and find a point of commonality. That's what networking is really. It's finding that point of commonality and taking the relationship from there."

"Strategic Stalking"

While stalking may seem like an aggressive term, Hannah explained that by stalking someone on Twitter what you are actually doing is "intelligence gathering." You learn about the person, and once you've learned something about the individual or company and what they're saying, you can then engage with them.

Madalyn agrees. "I just love that I can connect with people (on Twitter) that I don't think I would be able to connect with anywhere else." This is where Twitter really shines. It's also the thing most people don't understand about Twitter and what should make it the platform of choice for business professionals.

There are no gatekeepers on Twitter, meaning that if someone you want to meet—say a recruiter, hiring manager, or influencer in your industry—is active on Twitter, there's a great chance you can reach out to them and have a conversation.

Using Twitter to Build Your CareerKred

Now that you know Twitter is a great place to connect with people you may not be able to meet otherwise and you can facilitate those connections through intelligence gathering, the next question is: Why else would we want to use Twitter?

When I asked Mark Babbitt this question, here's what he had to say:

> One of the best parts about social media and especially Twitter [is that] anybody can have a Twitter account, and based on your niche, your field of expertise, you can express your feelings on a hot topic, or a trend with your industry. By doing this, you can establish subject matter expertise and become known as the expert.

Okay, now that we have an understanding of the platform and why we would want to use it, it's time to dive deeper and learn about how to set yourself up for success on Twitter before you send out your first tweet.

Here are four key items you must pay attention to as you setup your Twitter account.

Your Twitter Name and Handle

Just as with LinkedIn, your success on Twitter starts with how you set up your account. Doing it right allows you to establish your brand before you ever send out that first tweet. Too many people I work with have incomplete or inadequate Twitter profiles. If you want to connect, grow your network, and demonstrate your expertise, you need to take the platform seriously, starting with your Twitter handle.

This may seem trivial, but I assure you it will make a huge difference in your success on Twitter: The first thing you need to decide on when setting up your account is your name and your Twitter handle.

Your name is exactly what it sounds like. I recommend using your first and last name. If possible, it should be the same name you used when you purchased your domain. Your Twitter name will appear above your Twitter handle in your profile.

Once you've selected your Twitter username, it's time to select your Twitter handle. Your Twitter handle is what people will use to connect with and mention you. It's your "at (@)" handle.

It should come as no surprise, but I recommend using your first and last name as your @ handle. Madalyn Sklar agrees, saying, "I would absolutely use your first and last name." Remember, you are trying to build a comprehensive, cohesive, and congruent brand online. Using your name for all of your online activities helps Google link all of your accounts and distinguish you from others who share your name.

That's why it's important to use your first and your last name. Not teddybear238 or John117. Twitter is a conversation-based platform, and if you want to be taken seriously, you need to first take it seriously herself. Using an alias will not help you build your brand. Besides, what will the recruiter who just looked you up think when he or she sees that your Twitter handle is @ihatemyjob? That might be a catchy name as your Xbox gamer tag, but it won't win you any career-branding points.

Your Profile Picture

You also need a professional profile picture, just as you do with LinkedIn. Your profile picture is really important: It sets the tone, along with your name, for the impression you make on other people. Your image needs to convey your professionalism.

Katrina Collier, who sees hundreds if not thousands of profile pictures, told me the key to a good profile picture is "looking fabulous." She says, "You have a profile picture that represents you well, because that profile picture is public."

Katrina hits on another thing to keep in mind as you select your Twitter profile image: the fact that your image is searchable in Google. It's tied to your name, and anybody searching for you will see it in a

Google search result. Now how does that profile picture of you dressed in your Halloween costume sound?

If you're serious about building your brand and growing your CareerKred, I strongly encourage to consider the profile image you use. After all, it is your digital-first impression, so make sure you use a professional picture, and as a bonus, align it with your pictures on your other social media platforms. Congruency is key.

Your Bio

The next big ticket item for you to complete is your bio. Your bio should tell people who view it a little bit about yourself. Remember the biography exercise? In addition, for Twitter I recommend that you incorporate something that explains what people can expect to see from your tweets. Madalyn Sklar also believes a good bio could be the key to gaining followers:

> I'm very adamant on the importance of your Twitter bio. Your bio really sets the stage for your Twitter success. For example, if you sent out a tweet to me, and you're like, "Hey, @MadalynSklar, come check out me and my podcast," the first thing I'm going to do is go look at your bio so I can find out who this Ryan guy is and why I should I listen to him. It's amazing to me how many people out there put together really terrible Twitter bios.

Terrible twitter bios—we've all seen them, so we know exactly what Madalyn is talking about. I think where people go wrong with the Twitter bio is trying to fit too much into it without understanding the rules Twitter has set for the bio.

Your bio cannot exceed 160 characters. This means you want to use as much of that real estate as possible. The best use is to be transparent to your potential audience—you want to look like a real person, not a spammer. I admit, trying to fit your bio into 160 characters can be a chore, and it requires some thought on your part. This is why the Twitter bio was included as part of your career biography exercise.

If you're stuck on where to start, I suggest you go back and do the biography exercise, but in lieu of this, Katrina suggests taking a look at your headline on LinkedIn (congruency again coming into play). Other suggestions from both Madalyn and Katrina include using the keywords people would use in a Twitter search if they were looking for you.

In short, your bio should say to others: "Here's my face, here's who I am, and here's what I'm going to tweet about."

Your Banner Image

One of the most overlooked branding features for Twitter is the banner image. This is Twitter's way of helping you get past the 160-character limit in your bio and allow you to further brand yourself by making your banner image changeable.

The banner image is the large image at the top of your page. It's a big, panoramic image, and it's a good tool to help increase your brand awareness and help others identify with you and who you are.

You can create an image on sites like Canva or PicMonkey. The point is to expand on your brand using that image. If you have a book, show it. If you have spoken at an event, use an image from the event. The key here is to use a "success" image to convey to the person viewing your profile that you know what you're talking about.

That gets you set up. We'll talk later in the Engage step about how to use Twitter the right way to grow an audience and boost your CareerKred.

Exercise 13—Set Up Your Digital Assets

This exercise has two parts. For the first part, the social media audit, you will need the Social Media Accounts worksheet from the *CareerKred Workbook*. You can download the workbook at http://careerkredbook.com/workbook.

PART ONE

Using the worksheet labeled Your Digital Assets, list all of your current online social media and industry accounts. Provide your user name and the current bio in the spaces provided. This will put all of your accounts in place so you can easily identify needed changes or accounts that should be deleted.

PART TWO

Now it's time to set up your LinkedIn and Twitter accounts. Remember, this is not the place for incomplete profiles or selfie pictures. Both of these platforms are strategic to getting yourself integrated online in a way that will help get you discovered and recognized for your expertise, so take them both seriously.

LinkedIn: If you haven't already set up your a LinkedIn account, please do it now. There is a guided wizard waiting to help you. Follow the instructions on the screen and in this book to ensure you complete every section in a manner that will help build your brand.

Twitter: Even if you hate social media, as a business professional you need a Twitter account. We'll talk specifics a little later, but for now just know that Twitter plays an important role in helping you establish your brand online. So follow the steps outlined above and get ready to tweet your way to recognition.

The Integrate Step Checklist

- [ ] Take the Digital Brand Assessment (if not already completed)
- [ ] Score: ______________
- [ ] Conduct a digital audit

Step #1 - Your Career Story

- [ ] Complete the Career Biography worksheet
- [ ] Develop bios for social media

Step #2 - A Personal Website

- [ ] Identify the keywords you want to be known for
- [ ] Select how you want to build your website: DIY or DFY

  ____

- [ ] Identify your domain name

  ____

- [ ] Setup your website

Step #3 - Personal Brand Landing Pages

- [ ] Setup your Personal Brand Landing Pages

Step #4 - Social Media

- [ ] Setup your LinkedIn profile (Use bio from Career Story exercise)
- [ ] Setup your Twitter profile (Use bio from Career Story exercise)

Part Five

The Create Step

"Time is what we want most, but what we use worst."
—William Penn

Leverage your knowledge and expertise
to grow your influence.

Digital Brand Assessment Score: 51–75

Assessment takers with a score between fifty-one and seventy-five are more readily found in Google search and may have started creating content. These folks are typically in the Create step.

Even though you will be found in Google searches, the key to the Create Step is making sure you are found for what you want to be known for. When someone searches for you, will they be able to paint an accurate picture of who you are and what you are all about?

You have started to create a digital brand, and you recognize the importance of your personal brand. You might create content regularly, and you may even contribute to online question-and-answer sites.

For the most part, you have started taking control of your digital brand and online presence. Here are some common thoughts for people who find themselves with a score in this range.

1. I want to be recognized in my industry, niche, or area of expertise.
2. I want to become a thought leader.
3. I want to make better use of social media.
4. I need to find the right content to post online.
5. I need to find more time to create content.

Helping you gain answers to all of these thoughts is crux of the Create step. In order to continue boosting your CareerKred, you will need more and different content aligned with what you want to be known for. This requires exercising your idea muscle like never before.

Chapter 26

The Content Muscle

Many people have told me they want to be recognized as an expert in their niche. They want to be seen as thought leaders in their industry. If this describes you, creating and publishing relevant content is the key to getting recognized as an expert, a thought leader.

How else will people know what you are all about? Earlier, you identified what you want to be known for. Publishing content is how you make that happen. At this point, some of you might be voicing to yourselves (or maybe even out loud) the following:

"I can't write."
"I don't know what to write about."
"Why would anyone listen to me?"
"I don't have the time to create content."
"How do I write for a side business when I'm employed full-time?"

These are all valid concerns, but in reality they are mostly excuses. I get it, though. Writing is tough. But so is the first workout you do after being "off" for a while. However, if you stick with it, and you're consistent, the workouts become easier, and you're able to do more in the same amount of time. Writing is no different.

Claudia Altucher, author of the book *Become an Idea Machine in 180 Days*, introduced me to the concept of the Idea Muscle. Her thesis is that the brain is like a muscle. Specifically, it is an idea muscle. Of course this is figurative muscle, but as Claudia explained, it acts very much like the other more tangible muscles in our body.

To help you understand how the idea muscle works, take a few minutes and try this simple thought exercise. On a blank sheet of paper, write down the following:

- Your top ten favorite foods
- Your top ten all-time favorite movies
- The top ten apps you use the most on your phone (no peeking)
- Ten apps you'd like to use that have not yet been invented

Go ahead. I'll wait.

All done? How'd you do? If you're like me, you were probably able to list five to six pretty easily for each item, and then you hit a wall. Claudia explained that, at this point, your idea muscle is starting to sweat—just like that point in your exercise when your muscles start to scream at you to stop.

When you reached this point, I'm betting you were tempted to quit, weren't you? After all, it's just a simple exercise in a book; no need to exert yourself. However, in order to be successful at anything you do in life, whether it's getting healthier, writing down ten ideas, or publishing relevant content for your niche, you have to push through this resistance.

When Claudia's clients reach this point and are tempted to give up, she sends them back to list *twenty* ideas instead of ten. What can I say? She's hardcore.

But she is also absolutely correct. Yes, writing is hard. Yes, you will struggle and you will want to quit. When you reach this point you have to ask yourself, "How bad do I want it? Am I willing to put in the work required to become recognized for my expertise?" If not, you may as well close this book now.

If you are ready to do the work, if you're ready to exercise your idea muscle, then let's keep moving forward, and we'll push past the resistance together.

Create Step 1

Chapter 27

Getting Started

It all starts the first time you hit publish. If you want to establish your CareerKred, you need to hit publish. In order to hit publish, you need to blog.

We've covered the advantages that having a website gives you over your competition, but as a reminder, only 4 percent of business professionals have one, and only 1 percent of LinkedIn users actually hit the publish button.

Clearly blogging can set you apart. It also provides you with the opportunity to continue to be a Relentless Giver. But the most important part of blogging is giving your audience a chance to get to know you—what you know, how you think, and your communication style. This provides them with a better idea of who you are and what you are about. The only other way to glean this type of information about someone is to meet them face-to-face.

Trevor Young, author of the book *microDomination*, also believes in the power of blogging. Trevor told me during our interview that blogging says so much about you as a person. Not only does blogging help you clarify your own thoughts, but it also "signifies to (to others) that you are showing up, that you care, you want to share, and you want to be generous."

Sounds like a Relentless Giver, eh?

Earlier I listed the common excuses I hear from people about why they can't hit the publish button. The most common excuse is they don't know what they would write about. I completely understand this position. I was there, too, when I first started out.

In order to help you overcome this mindset—and it *is* a mindset—what follows are some suggestions on topics to help you get started.

Three Topics to Get You Started Blogging

As you get started blogging, it's important to remember the purpose behind it. In addition to sharing your knowledge, you want to become known for knowing something. So it stands to reason that your blog posts should be all about whatever that something is.

But you can't post content just for the sake of posting content. You need to write about the things that are important and relevant to you within your industry. You should have captured some of this during the Define step. If you didn't, and you're starting to really think about it now, here are a few ideas to get you started.

I Know What You Did Last Weekend

What did you do over the weekend? What books did you read, what websites did you visit? If you could do anything in your spare time, what would it be? I'm asking because the answers to all of these questions are indicators of where your passions may lie.

Take me, for example. I write about personal branding, online reputation management, and career-related topics. But before I wrote a single word, I was reading about these topics in books and blog posts.

I also observed that coworkers—and sometimes strangers—would ask me for career advice or for assistance with updates to their resumes. I was doing all of these things "naturally," so when I took the time to understand what I wanted to be known for, the logical choice was to merge them all together and start publishing my thoughts.

My wife looks at real estate and vacation rentals in her spare time. I merely need to mention a new location as a possible vacation spot, and within thirty minutes she has found the perfect place to stay. She's also researched airfare costs, the best restaurants in the area, and the most popular places to visit. I've suggested many times that she should consider becoming a real estate or travel agent. While she shrugs off this notion, what if she started blogging about vacation ideas, vacation trips, and real estate in certain areas of the country or the world?

Would you like to go to Tahiti? My wife could provide a great itinerary quickly. Every possible trip, vacation, or house for sale is a potential new blog post. If she started doing this, she would be helping others while pursuing her passion. Again, the definition of a Relentless Giver.

If she continued this on a consistent basis, she would eventually become known within the travel industry, and more importantly, others would start to like and trust her advice. She would be well on her way to becoming "known for knowing something," as Jane Anderson would say.

So what about you? What do you enjoy? Fishing? Camping? Accounting? Engineering? Product management? Do you help start-up companies? Do you get excited about career development or personal training?

Whatever it is that gets you excited, whatever turns a "I'll just look this up" moment into an hour or more behind a computer, that can become the subject of your blog. The best part? Every time you hit publish, you'll be demonstrating your knowledge and expertise by helping others.

What Do People Ask You About?

Think about what people regularly ask you about? What topics do they come to you for advice on? Are you the techie go-to person within your circle of friends?

Chances are, if people are asking you about a specific topic, it means you have already built some CareerKred on that topic, and they value your opinion. They may even see you as an expert on said topic.

When I started paying attention to what people were asking me about, I noticed they were coming to me for advice on career opportunities, career development, resumes, personal branding, and online reputation management.

Why? Because I've had real experiences with each of those topics. Am I an all-knowing expert on all things career or personal branding? No way. But I do know more about those topics than most, so people look to me as a go-to resource.

This is what blogging and putting yourself "out there" can do for you. It helps position you as the leader in your field, as someone who can be trusted for advice and insights.

Think about it for a minute. What topics do others look to you as the go-to resource for? And don't say "nothing." We all have some topic or subject of interest where we know more than others. You just may not see it that way yet. But you will.

Discover what topic people come to you the most for, and then write about it. Take some time over the next couple of days to pay attention when people approach you. Listen to what they ask you about. What questions do you answer for them without even thinking about your response? Uncover these topics—and then go hit publish.

What Do You Want to Be Known For?

This is the most important question of all, and frankly, it gets to the heart of this book. *What do you want to be known for?* If you followed the exercises in the Define step, you should already know the answer to this question.

But let's say that, even after completing the exercises, you're still stuck or unsure. For fun, let's assume you're a program manager, but you secretly want to become a basketball coach. In this scenario, it's very possible for you to maintain your employment while pursuing your basketball dream on the side. Since this is a complete career change for you, you definitely need to build up your CareerKred.

Blogging moves you in this direction.

Have you developed any basketball plays? What practices have you put together? Write about and publish them on your website. Did you read an article about an officiating change that you disagreed with or that helped you form a new opinion? Consider writing a contradictory or an agreement post about your take on the change.

People love to read about the journey, so why not take them along with you?

Write about how you identified your skills gaps and your plan to narrow or eliminate those gaps. Are there trainings, conferences, or seminars you can attend to gain skills and move closer to what you want to be known for? Blog about your experiences along the way. Don't hold anything back—share your frustrations, your setbacks, and of course, your victories. By being honest and relevant, people will learn from your mistakes. You'll inspire and encourage them. They'll say to themselves, "If he (she) can do it, well, I can do that too." You are becoming a Relentless Giver.

But nothing happens if you don't hit publish.

Embrace Anonymity

Another reason people hesitate to get started writing a blog is they are secretly afraid of what others might think. To be honest, I still struggle with this. You know what helps me? Publishing.

The reality is that, in the beginning no one will read your content. Virtually no one, anyway. Sound depressing? Well, it's true. Unless you are Richard Branson or some other already famous person, when you start you will not have an audience.

I tell you this not to scare you off, but to help you set realistic expectations. You will not get a thousand people to read your very first blog post, and this is a actually a good thing. Instead of obsessing about what people will think about your writing or your thoughts on a topic, embrace the gift of anonymity.

Use this initial time of "invisibility" to hone your writing style, discover the best time of day for writing, and develop your thoughts on your topics or area of interest. The key is to keep hitting publish; keep exercising your content-creation muscle. Each time you publish, you will grow as a person and a writer. Your thoughts will become clearer and so will your focus.

When I first started blogging, I wrote about woodworking. I was an avid woodworker at the time. I devoured articles, magazines, and books—and I could never get enough of Norm from *This Old House.* For the longest time, not a weekend would go by without me working in the garage on some new woodworking project, whether it was shelves, cabinets, or tables, to name a few.

I published articles about my process, the wood I used, and the reasons I selected it. The tools I used, the table saw, the planer, the drill press, and even the sandpaper I bought all became subjects for blog posts. I even posted my handwritten plans for the furniture I made.

It was a great outlet for me, but more importantly, I learned it was OK to publish.

Exercise 14—The Content Muscle

This exercise will help you get past another common objection: the "I don't know what to write about" objection. You can download the Content Muscle worksheet from the *CareerKred Workbook* at http://careerkredbook.com/workbook.

This will benefit you in a couple of ways. First, it will get you thinking about topics in the area you want to become known for. Second, and borrowing from Claudia, it will get you to start flexing your idea muscle.

With this in mind, I want to you to capture on paper your ideas for the following subjects. Pay particular attention to the quantities for each.

The top ten websites you regularly visit
The last ten books you read
Ten topics in your industry that interest you
Ten things you love about your industry
Ten things you would improve about your industry
Ten topics that run parallel to your industry
Ten people you admire or look to as a mentor in your industry
Ten topics your industry mentors have written about in the last month
Ten ways you agree or disagree with your industry mentors
Ten conferences or trade shows in your industry

It's a lot, I know. However, if you can complete this exercise, not only will you have flexed your content muscle, you will have also come up with one hundred ideas for potential blog posts. Pretty cool, eh? You officially no longer have any excuses.

Thank you, Claudia, for the gift of the Idea Muscle.

Chapter 28

Content Defined

As you think about publishing content on your blog, keep in mind that today content is not one-dimensional. Up to this point, I've only discussed written content, but there are other types of content you can use to grow your CareerKred as well.

I probably should have defined this earlier, but before we go on any further, I want to make sure we are on the same page when I refer to content.

> Content is the written, visual, audio, and video information you publish on the Web to share your knowledge and expertise with your audience.

This definition captures pretty much everything about content. A shorter version of the same definition would be: Content is anything you post online.

Content can be in the form of posts, videos, presentations, images, audio files, podcasts, eBooks, pdfs, and so on. The *medium* you choose doesn't matter so much; what matters is the *message*.

As you work to build your brand in a specific area or niche, you must publish relevant content. Content creation is where the rubber hits the road, so to speak. It pulls together everything we've discussed up to this point in the book.

Content creation is where the Define and Integrate steps combine so people begin to get to know and like you. Content creation is where your keyword research, knowledge of your niche, and your personality all come together to produce informative and entertaining content written specifically to educate your audience.

Off-Brand versus On-Brand

One thing to keep in mind as you create and post content online is that everything you post is a reflection of your brand—everything. That selfie of you at the party last weekend tells a story. The comment you left on Facebook about a political issue tells a story too. Everything you post online gets sifted through and collated by people who do not yet know you. This information is then rewritten, if you will, in their minds, creating their own story about you—even if it's not the story you want them to tell.

Jeff Bezos, CEO of Amazon, once famously said, "Your brand is what people say about you when you are not in the room."[11] So true, and even more true as people review your online profile. The content you post goes a long way towards shaping the impression people form about you even if you never meet them in person.

When you are beginning the Create step, it's important to keep this in mind and remember that you are building a brand, not a collection of unrelated, random stuff. That's why, at least for a while, everything you post online should be "on-brand." At the very least, you should seriously consider what you post as it relates to the brand you are trying to build.

On-brand simply means staying consistent and congruent with your posts. They should all revolve around your topic, subject, or niche. If you feel the need to post a selfie, make sure it is one of you at a conference, tradeshow, or hanging with your coworkers after a long day at work. This will keep your need to post to Instagram in check, while at the same time adding CareerKred to your brand.

Remaining on-brand will not only build your brand faster, it also will keep people from being confused when they find you online for the first time. Remember, in today's digital age you are making a first impression even while you sleep.

Is it ever OK to go "off-brand"?

The short answer is yes; however, you must do so wisely. Posts that help display your personal side, for example, can be beneficial when building your brand. Posts showing you with your dog, your significant

---

11 Fifield, A. (2014) 9 Killer quotes from the world's top billionaires. Retrieved from http://addicted2success.com/quotes/9-killer-branding-quotes-from-the-worlds-top-billionaires/#.

other, vacations you've taken, and even hanging with your family over a holiday are all good for helping people decipher who you are. These types of post complement your brand.

True off-brand posts, in my opinion, generally fall into three big categories: sex, politics, and religion. Politics is where most people go off-brand. They get on Facebook and respond to a post that conflicts with their own beliefs, and before you know it, the response turns into a rant—a rant, mind you, that can damage your brand and your reputation.

Now before you get all "my Facebook account is private" or "it's my right to post whatever I want to my account," I'll stipulate that you are correct. However, it also might be the "right" of hiring managers, recruiters, and potential employers to take your comments as offensive and move on to someone else.

If that last paragraph is offensive to you, take a step back and look at it objectively. If you're trying to build a brand, is it worth the off-brand post just for you to make a point? I don't think so, but ultimately it's up to you to decide.

Warren Buffett, founder of Berkshire Hathaway, once said, "It takes twenty years to build a reputation and five minutes to ruin it. If you think about that, you'll do things differently."

The same is true today, except you can build your brand and reputation much faster than twenty years, and you can lose it in a matter of seconds. When building your brand, it is best to stay away from controversial or divisive off-brand topics such as sex, politics, and religion.

Unless, of course, one those topics is what you want to be known for, in which case the more controversial and divisive, the better for growing an audience. But for the rest of you, it's better to stay on-brand and on-topic.

Chapter 29

The Content Pyramid

Now that you understand the basics, I want to introduce you to the concept of the Content Pyramid. The pyramid is something I conceived after taking a step back and looking at what was happening in the world of content marketing.

From the earlier definition, you already know that content can be written, visual, audio, or video. But which do you use? Understanding the type of content to to use starts by collecting and organizing your thoughts and then asking yourself, "Where does my audience reside? Are they on YouTube? Instagram? Websites? Do they listen to podcasts?" Answering these questions will help you understand which of the different types of content you should use.

However, not all content is created equal. Some types of content require a lot more time, effort, and cost to produce. I developed the Content Pyramid with this in mind. As you move up the pyramid to each of the different types of content, the amount of work on your part goes up as well.

While it still takes time to produce, written content is the least cost-prohibitive and in my opinion is the basis for everything you do online.

Written Content

Personally, I believe regardless of the content format you choose, everything starts with writing. It forms the base of the pyramid. Why? Because if you want high quality, relevant audio, images, or video, before you press the record or upload button, you need to consider what you're going to say.

Every post tells a story, and all stories come to life through writing. Do you think your favorite celebrities ad lib their lines on camera? Of course they don't. They generally read from a written script in order to maintain the storyline.

I should note here that if they do ad lib, it's usually in line with the character they are portraying. The off-script comments don't detract from the characters brand; instead, they serve to enhance it by staying on brand.

Written content requires you to write out your thoughts digitally or on paper. (Any old schoolers out there?) How you do this or what app you use doesn't matter. You can create written content directly in your WordPress post if you like.

Personally, I create my content in a third-party app, usually Google Docs, and then I paste it into a WordPress post. This prevents me from accidentally posting content that is not quite ready. You know, full of typos and run-on sentences.

One of the hidden benefits of written content is the ability to include the keywords you researched and identified in earlier exercises.

Keywords help search engines understand what your post is about, and it's keywords that will determine if your posts turn up in search results. A word of caution on keywords: Don't over use them in your post. Google frowns on this practice.

It is worth mentioning that search engine optimization (SEO) is beyond the scope for this book. If you are interested in learning more about SEO best practices, I recommend that you contact Todd Lohenry (toddlohenry.com). Todd was one of my podcast guests and is very knowledgeable about all things SEO. I recommend checking out his work.

While SEO is out of scope, here are four keyword placement best practices to follow when composing your posts:

1. Include keywords in your post title.
2. Use keywords in the subtitles within your post.
3. Use your keywords in the body of your post.
4. Use keywords in the images in your posts.

Another best practice to keep in mind as you write your post is using natural language. In other words, use language your audience understands by speaking like a person, not like a bot. Use variations of your keywords—or alternatives, if appropriate—within the post body. Stick with these basic rules of thumb and your posts are sure to rise to the top of a Google search.

As I said at the beginning, written content forms the base of your Content Pyramid. It provides you with well-thought-out, educational material that will not only help educate or inform your audience but also positions you as the Relentless Giver in your niche.

Sitting on top written content is a relatively new layer, at least in Internet years, that has quickly become a driving force for views and traffic on the Internet. I'm talking about visual content—specifically images.

Image Content

Images have always existed on the Internet. In my humble opinion, images make the Internet. Without them the Internet would be more of a utilitarian place versus a place where people spend countless hours of their time.

Think about it. How much time would you spend surfing the Net if there were no images?

Because of their importance in making the Net go round, I place images as the next layer on the Content Pyramid. They can also cost a little more to generate and they can take more time, depending on the type of images you are creating.

Images can be used in conjunction with other content in order to explain or further illustrate a point. Blog posts, for example, are a great place for you to post images to complement or enhance your post.

Because of their rise in prominence, there has been an equal rise in applications, both on the Web and on your smartphone to help you develop the perfect image. When I create images for a post, I generally use Canva, but I have been known to use PicMonkey as well. Both do a great job of helping develop an image for a post or a specific platform. If you need an image for Facebook, there's a template. Instagram, they have you covered as well.

For the most part, using these tools is free unless you want to take advantage of premium offers, in which case you'll pay to use that particular service. The same is true for image apps on your smartphone.

I currently use a few apps on my phone to varying degrees of success. I use WordSwag and occasionally Over to put added text with my images. This makes me feel like I'm a typography expert. I also use an app called Pic Stitch in order to join multiple photos into one.

Two other apps I use are Snapseed for editing (it's owned by Google, and I don't think there is a better photo editing app out there) and Juxtaposer for creating transparent, layered images.

If you're going to go slightly off-brand, the images layer on the Content Pyramid is where you should do it. Images can be used to get more "personal" with your audience. You can use them to show your likes, such as food preferences or clothing styles. Or you can use them to show behind the scenes views of your office, your car, your favorite sports team, or your pet.

The images layer is the most versatile layer on the Content Pyramid. The key is to use them to show off your personality and connect with your audience on a more personal level. Speaking of getting more personal, the next layer on the Content Pyramid is Audio.

Audio Content

According to an article on TheAtlantic.com, "audio is one of the most intimate forms of media (content) because you are constantly building your own images of the story in your mind."[12]

Consider that for minute. Think about the last time your were listening to a podcast, perhaps The *BRAND New You Show*. As you were listening, could you visualize what the host or guest was talking about in your mind? I personally do it all the time, and this is exactly why audio—specifically podcasts—has grown exponentially over the last couple of years.

---

12 Wen, T (2015) Inside the podcast brain: Why do audio stories captivate? Retrieved from http://www.theatlantic.com/entertainment/archive/2015/04/podcast-brain-why-do-audio-stories-captivate/389925/.

Audio is the third layer in the Content Pyramid. You could argue that images may take more time and effort, but when I think of audio, I'm thinking about podcasts or other recordings found on various social media platforms.

Just as it sounds, audio content requires you to capture your content using an audio-recording device such as your phone. If you have an iPhone, the native voice memo app works great for this. There are many other options available for your phone as well—just search for "audio recorder" on iTunes or the Google Play store.

Phone apps are a great way to get started in audio, but keep in mind that while phone apps work, they are limited in functionality and can be of lower quality. As a general rule of thumb, they will pick up all ambient noise in addition to the voices you want to be heard. So if audio quality is important to you—and it should be—you'll want to consider some alternatives.

The next step up in capturing audio is to use a microphone and record into either your computer or your phone. Microphones can range from twenty dollars to hundreds of dollars. The choice of microphone is a personal one, but don't get too hung up on getting the perfect one out of the gate. Just get one and get started.

Regardless of how you record your audio or what device you use, you will need to make sure your audio content fits the needs to your audience. This may mean that you'll need to script out your audio before recording it. That's what I do.

Writing out your script allows you to review it before you hit record. Speaking of hitting record, the last type of content in the Content Pyramid is video. Video is quickly rising in the ranks for driving Internet traffic.

Video Content

Video. Video. Video. Depending on which article you read, video will drive up to 84 percent of all Internet traffic by 2018. In 2016 three hundred hours of video was uploaded to YouTube every minute. Read that again: Every. Minute.

Videos are a great way to show off your brand and connect with people on a personal level. Video picks up where audio leaves off. A video allows you to share your story visually, which, judging by the popularity of vlogs, is something the public craves. To say the use of video for content is exploding is a tremendous understatement. I don't need to look any further than my youngest son to grasp the impact video is having on our world.

Like audio content, video is now relatively easy to produce since every smartphone comes equipped with a camera. But just because it's easy doesn't mean it's good.

Producing video content can be as easy as opening an app on your phone, switching to the front-facing camera and pressing record. When finished you can upload it to YouTube in a matter of seconds or minutes depending on length and Internet connection.

There's a bonus with video content most people don't think about: YouTube. YouTube is the second-largest search engine in the world, and Google owns it. For this reason alone, you should strongly consider creating a YouTube channel.

Obviously, video content can quickly scale in cost, time, and effort depending on the quality level you require. This will be different for each of us, but as you create video content, keep in mind that people can tolerate a relatively bad video as long as it is engaging. If the audio is bad, however, they will tune out quickly.

I would be remiss if I didn't mention live streaming as a video medium as well. Live streaming is exactly what it sounds like: broadcasting yourself or your surroundings live, in real time. Apps like Periscope and Facebook Live make live streaming possible.

To do it, you simply open the app, give your broadcast a title, click the broadcast button, and start talking. A word of caution about these platforms, though—they really do broadcast LIVE, so be careful what you stream. It can be super easy for you to go off-brand here.

I have tried live streaming in the past. I was on Periscope (which I predict will be known as Twitter Live eventually) the day it launched. It makes me uncomfortable, however—mostly because I rely so heavily on the written word and I don't tend to carry cue cards around with me. But for some, live streaming is a very natural thing. If this is you, my hat is off to you.

Chapter 30

Writing as a Full-Time Employee

I often hear concerns from podcast listeners, blog readers, and even via email about posting content while working a full-time job or when working a full-time job and running a business on the side. This is a legitimate concern, and one I am familiar with because I have a full-time job as well.

First, let me say I completely get where you are coming from. As you start building your brand, or before you start your side business, my advice is to take the time to read your company's conflict of interest policy. If your company has a policy on social media or other Internet related activities, read those as well.

If you're in doubt about your company's Internet-related policies, find someone in your company to ask. Doing so will not only keep you out of trouble, it may also give you the confidence you need to get started—because when it comes to your job, which is most likely supporting your business in the beginning, it's better to be safe than sorry. There is no asking for forgiveness later.

Speaking of asking for forgiveness, never use company resources or company time to conduct your side business. This should be a no-brainer, but you never know. When I travel for work, I carry two laptops and two cell phones—one for business and the other for personal use. I recommend doing the same.

The more you can separate your full-time job from your part-time business, the better off you will be. Once you've disclosed your business or you've been given the green light to proceed, make sure your posts don't include company information or other references to what is happening within your company. Leave out your company's competitors as well.

If your side business is in direct conflict with your full-time job, you will need to make a decision on which one you want to pursue, or someone else might make that decision for you.

If, on the other hand, your side business and the products and services you provide are completely unrelated to your day job, then most likely you are in the clear. Choose your content type and publish away.

Chapter 31

Are You a Consumer or a Creator?

I believe there are two types of people in this world: creators and consumers. Creators change the world; consumers observe it. Creators add real value to others; consumers talk about and often criticize the value of the creators.

This may seem harsh at first, but it's something I've seen with my own eyes every day as I've worked to build the framework for the DICE process.

All of us—yes, you too—are experts at something. We have skills, acquired over months and years of hard work and effort. Unfortunately we are hesitant to share those skills with others because we lack confidence in our abilities and we don't receive positive acknowledgment from others about those skills.

The Define step in the DICE has been developed to help you see and grasp the depth of your skills, knowledge, and expertise. The Integrate step helps to position you online as a Relentless Giver so you can share your expertise with the world.

While both are powerful steps toward giving you the confidence you need to see yourself as an expert, the two steps combined will not get others to acknowledge your expertise. Calling yourself an expert is one thing, but when someone else calls you an expert, that's something entirely different.

Creating content will cause others to view you as an expert.

Leonardo da Vinci is arguably the most famous artist and sculptor to have ever walked the face of the earth. He is the ultimate creator. His masterpieces still attract millions of visitors every year, and his brilliance can be seen in his work—even the works he started but never finished.

As you might think, it took Leonardo years to hone his craft, just like it has taken you years to develop your skills and expertise. But what if instead of creating, Leonardo spent those same years consuming? Rather than putting brush to canvas, what if he had decided to watch others do it instead? What if, instead of putting hammer to marble, he chose to read about how others had done it in the past?

If Leonardo had taken this approach to his art and his sculpting, what are the chances that we would know who Leonardo is today? The answer is virtually none, and this is the difference between a creator and a consumer.

Leonardo has been credited with the following quote that I believe captures the difference between creators and consumers perfectly:

> It had long since come to my attention that people of accomplishment rarely sat back and let things happen to them. They went out and happened to things.

"They went out and happened to things": This is a common theme among the people I have spoken to both on my podcast and in person. If you look closely at the background of those that get ahead, those that get the position or role they want, you will see at some point in their career story they choose to create, not consume. Leonardo also said:

> I have been impressed with the urgency of doing. Knowing is not enough; we must apply. Being willing is not enough; we must do.

"We must do." Sounds like something Yoda would say, but wise words nonetheless. This is especially true in today's work environment; knowing is not enough. If you want to be recognized as an expert, as the go-to person in your niche (which is, by the way, where the top earners in your niche currently reside), you must create something. You have to take your expertise and apply it in some way for the benefit of others.

The Way We Work Is Changing

We are rapidly approaching the year 2020. Earlier I mentioned that by the year 2020 an estimated 40 percent of the global workforce will be freelancers. That means four out of ten of you reading this book right now will be working for themselves and selling their skills and expertise to companies, either as a consultant or a creator.

A study by PriceWaterhouseCoopers found that two out of five (40 percent) of HR professionals believe that "traditional employment won't be around in the future. Instead, people will have their own 'brands' and sell their skills to those who need them."[13]

Those same HR professionals are already making this a reality, because 31 percent of them, according to the same study, have already started "building their talent strategies around the rise of the portfolio career, hiring a diverse mix of people on an affordable, ad hoc basis."

If this is true, I believe the year 2020 will also bring about the beginning of the end of the resume and thus the job search process as we know it today. As opposed to bullet points on a piece of paper, companies will look for real-world examples of your accomplishments. The executive summary of the modern resume will become the About page on your website.

Why I am telling you this, you ask? Simple. Those of you who grasp this concept, who see the world of work changing right before your eyes, will realize that the key to employment in the not-so-distant future is to be recognized and acknowledged by others as the expert, the go-to person in your niche. You will have demonstrable CareerKred. Content creation has the power to get you there . . . but only if you have the courage to create.

You need to put yourself out there and share your knowledge with the world, comfortable with knowing that you are not giving away all of your secrets but instead planting the seeds for your future successes. Surviving this freelance economy will require you to become a creator, a Relentless Giver. Start now to help others through your actions because, as Leonardo said, knowing is not enough. In the

---

13 Rendell, M. & Brown, J. (2105). The Future of Work a Journey to 2022, 23. Retrieved from http://www.pwc.com/gx/en/issues/talent/future-of-work/journey-to-2022.html.

corporate world knowledge used to be power. The people that had it stayed at the top. It was the lack of knowledge that held one back in many cases.

This not true today. Knowledge is accessible to everyone; it has become a commodity. But what is not a commodity and never will be is the Relentless Giver mindset. This is the key to your future job satisfaction and success.

Give your knowledge away through your actions, and others will take notice. As Leonardo said, you must apply. You must do. To become a Relentless Giver, you need to adopt the mindset of a creator and abandon the consumer mindset that in all likelyhood, has been reinforced in you since you first started your career.

Content creation takes courage, perseverance, and mettle. But if you develop the courage to become a creator, I promise you, your brand and your future will be different than you imagine them today.

Every time you publish content, someone will take notice. With each new piece of content you produce, you establish yourself as a thought leader. People will begin to recognize your expertise, and they may even recommend you to others for information and knowledge in your niche.

But this only happens when you act, when you do, and when you create. So before you say you can't write or you're concerned about what others might think, take a minute and consider where Leonardo Da Vinci would be today if he had decided to consume rather than create.

Exercise 15—Become a Creator

In this exercise, you are going to flip the switch in your mind and go from being a consumer to becoming a creator. If you're still hesitant to put yourself out there, please reread the last section. I believe that your career depends on it.

Use the Exercise 15 worksheet to complete this exercise. You can find it in the *CareerKred Workbook* at http://careerkredbook.com/workbook.

Go back to the last exercise, Your Content Muscle, and pull from your list of topics one that you are passionate about. Once you've selected your topic, sit down and write about it.

Don't worry about grammar, spelling, or publishing styles. Just write. Express all your thoughts, ideas, and feelings on the topic. When you're finished, save it and put it away for future use.

Doing this will allow you to clear your mind, which in turn will open it up to new possibilities. It will also allow your content idea muscle time to relax.

The next day, go back and read what you wrote. Review it for grammar and spelling. Review it for context. Once you've finished editing it, copy and paste your text into an online tool called Polish My Writing. This application will take care of any spelling and grammar errors you may have missed. Now you can be confident what you put out there is correct, grammatically speaking.

After completion, log into your website, copy and paste your post, and click the publish button. Congratulations! You've just taken the first step to becoming a creator.

Create Step 2

Chapter 32

Repurpose Your Time

Right after "I don't know what I want to write about," "I don't have enough time" is the excuse I hear most often from my clients during the Create step. When I hear this, I always ask about the client's long-term goals. Not the client's goal for next quarter—as a society we focus too much on the short term. Instead, I ask about where they want to be five years. How about you? Where do you see yourself in five years? If you worked through the Define step, you can not only answer this question, you can also tell me the things you need to do in order to get there.

Stephen Covey once said, "The key is not to prioritize what's on your schedule, but to schedule your priorities."[14] It's a subtle but simple shift in a mindset that plagues us all. We get so wrapped up in today and tomorrow that we forget about where we want to be next year and the year after that.

Keeping in mind your goals, always remember that you are building your brand so you can become recognized for your expertise. Creating content accelerates this, so it pays to make the time to create it.

Developing content takes time, but time is an interesting thing. It's the only real constant in the universe. Regardless of where you live in the world, you only get 168 hours every week. The math is easy, but what you do with those hours sometimes is not.

---

14 Kruse, K. (2012) Stephen Covey: 10 Quotes that can change your life. Retrieved from http://www.forbes.com/sites/kevinkruse/2012/07/16/the-7-habits/#cbb0bd527051.

Exercise 16—Repurpose Your Time

For some of you, before you can even think about creating content, you must get past the mindset of not having enough time. I know because I've been there. When I started my blog, I thought I didn't have enough time either. Yet somehow during that first year of blogging, I was able to post sixty-two articles.

In addition to time being a constant in and of itself, time also allows you the freedom to do with it as you please. You can choose to spend an hour on Facebook. You can choose to spend an hour watching your favorite TV show. Or you can choose to spend that same time working on boosting your CareerKred. I choose the latter. I hope you do as well.

For this exercise, I want you to document what you do with your time this week. Write it down it a notebook, capture it on your calendar, or use the Repurpose Your Time worksheet in the *CareerKred Workbook*. You can download the worksheet at http://careerkredbook.com/workbook.

How you do it doesn't matter. What does matter is that you see how you use your time in any given week. Capture the time you watch TV, your commute time, and the time you spend on Facebook or other social media platforms. I could go on, but I think you get the point.

At the end of the week, take a good, hard look at where you currently spend your time. Ask yourself: "Instead of an hour on Facebook, what if I only spent a half hour and used the other half hour to write a blog post?"

During your commute, do you listen to the radio or the local talk show? Why not listen to a podcast or a "book on tape" instead? Turn your commute into a mobile university. The entire point of this exercise is understanding what you do with your time today and how you can repurpose it to begin to work on your future. I know you can do it. But you will need to schedule your priorities in order to make it happen.

Chapter 33

Repurpose Your Content

We've already established how important it is to repurpose your time in order to find the time to create content. Now it's time to look at how you can do the same with the content you create in order to maximize it.

Repurposing is simply the act of adapting something, whether it's time or content, for a different purpose. With time, you looked at where you spend your time through the week and compared those hours with your long-term objectives. Hopefully you made the decision to adapt the time not spent focusing on your long-term goals and align that time with your objectives.

Now you're going to do the same with the content you produce. You're going to take one piece of content you created in one medium and adapt it for use in another medium.

I know from experience that you need to be productive during your limited hours. This is especially true if you are building a side business while working a full-time job. Knowing how to make your content work for you is critical to growing your audience, your side business, and your CareerKred more quickly.

In order to achieve maximum productivity from your content, you need to see to it that every piece of content you produce has multiple lives. In fact, as you are creating and editing a piece of content, you should consider the different ways that content can be used.

To help this mindset sink in, the following is a list of ways you can repurpose your content by type, starting with written content. I should point out here that there are literally hundreds of ways to repurpose your content. What follows is great starting point, but it is not intended to be an exhaustive list.

Repurposing Your Written Content

As I mentioned before, for me everything in content creation starts with written content. Writing out my content helps me unpack my thoughts and organize them in a way that makes sense to me.

As you get started with content creation, I recommend you start with writing as well, and then move to other types of content as you get more comfortable with being "out there." That said, what else can you do with that great blog post you just released on your website? Here are a few suggestions.

Create Quote Images

I don't know about you, but I love reading quotes from people. I don't even really care who the quote is from as long as it is relevant. That's why I recommend creating quote images from your blog posts.

To do this, review your post and look for two to three great snippets or sentences you can turn into a quote. These quotes should highlight the main points of your post. Once you have identified the quotes you want to use, head over to Canva.com, PicMonkey.com, or your favorite phone app.

To get started, select one of the preformatted images for an Instagram post. Select a background image you feel captures the essence of your post, choose a font, and then superimpose your quote over the picture. Rearrange the words as you see fit, and once you are satisfied with your image, save it and post it to Instagram.

But wait! There's more. Before you leave Canva or PicMonkey, take the exact same image you just created and create another image for use on Facebook, Twitter, Google Plus, and LinkedIn.

Every time you post to a new platform, remember to provide a sentence or two describing what the post is about and why people would want to read it. For maximum exposure, add some relevant hashtags and the URL link back to your site.

Use Infographics

Infographics are all the rage today, so why not take advantage of them? Hannah Morgan, who wrote the book *The Infographic Resume*, introduced this concept to me as a way to "repurpose" your resume. You can do the same with your blog posts.

An infographic is simply a visual image used to represent data or information. You see them a lot online and especially on Pinterest. For example, if your blog post is about the top ten things you need to build your digital brand, an infographic for this post would have ten sections, each with a visual representation of the numbered item.

If item one of the top ten things was to buy your domain, you could show a graphic using www or an HTML graphic: </>. If item two was a website, you would show an image of a computer with a website on the screen, and so on.

Admittedly, creating an infographic is a little involved, but as is usually the case with a rising platform, there has also been a rise in companies and websites willing to help you create one. With a quick Google search, you can find infographic templates online at places such as Canva.com, Piktochart.com, and infographictemplates.com.

Create a Slideshare Presentation

Did you know that Slideshare.net is owned by LinkedIn? It is a hidden gem in the LinkedIn portfolio. I first heard about Slideshare from Matthew Capala, who was using it with great success to share content with his audience. Slideshare is basically an online repository for presentations. Once you have written a blog post, take a few minutes to put together a slideshow with lots of great visuals and your highlighted talking points.

Put Together a White Paper

Another thing you can do with your blog posts is string a few of them together to create a white paper. A white paper is a more formal piece of content that is highly relevant to your audience. If it helps, think of a white paper as a case study.

You use a white paper to walk the reader through complex issues or challenges they are facing, usually ending with a success story. A white paper helps people identify with the problem being discussed, gain some additional insight into the problem, and learn how to solve it. A white paper will typically have client or influencer testimonials or quotes included as well.

Refresh Older Content

Once you've been blogging for awhile, go through some of your older blog posts and breathe new life into them by refreshing them. This refresh can include adding more relevant images, updating the content with latest trends or statistics, or adding new links and updating older ones. You can even take the time to create new images and repost them to your social media accounts.

Create an Audio File

If you have a post that receives a lot of views, it might be a good idea to grab your favorite recording device and record yourself reading your post. Once finished, this will leave you with an audio file that you can add to your post as a download, upload to iTunes as a podcast, or put on Clammr, the audio snippet platform.

Create a Video

Turn on your camera and record yourself reading your blog post. When finished you will have a video you can post to YouTube. You can choose to upload the file directly to YouTube, or you can edit it using third-party software. Either way, you will have repurposed your written content into a video.

Create a Video Live Stream

You can also live stream yourself reading your blog. This avenue may or may not work for you depending on your feelings about live video. If you're hesitant, I recommend sticking with a video recording until you get comfortable behind the camera.

As you can see, there are multiple ways you can repurpose written content, which is why I say all content starts with writing. However, I know there are more than a few of you reading this who don't like writing. For you, I recommend starting with audio content.

Repurposing Your Audio Content

As a podcaster, I'm a little biased toward audio. However, even for me, everything starts with writing. If I'm going to publish a solo show, I write everything out first. I might ad lib a little during the recording, but for the most part, what I write is what I speak.

I do know many fellow podcasters, though, who do not write out anything at all. They turn on the mic and starting talking. The only thing they know in advance is the topic they will be speaking about.

A quick note on audio content: If you remember our discussion about the Content Pyramid, the further you climb up the pyramid, the more technically challenging your content creation becomes. In some cases, such as podcast production, it can start to get expensive as well. That said, there is no right or wrong way to create audio content, but once you have it, you can repurpose it in a number of ways.

Create a Written Blog Post

Recording content directly into the microphone gives you the beginnings of a blog post. After you've recorded yourself, you can have the audio file transcribed. Whenever I transcribe an audio file, I use a service called Rev.com. They charge a dollar a minute, but they are fast and very good. The files comes back to you in the form of a Microsoft Word document that you can easily edit (or not) and post directly to your website.

Rev.com even has an audio recording app that allows you to record your blog post directly into the app. Once you've finished, you click upload, and Rev.com will automatically transcribe your recording.

One thing to keep in mind as you read through these various repurposing methods: Whenever you get back to a written form of your content, everything I mentioned about repurposing it applies again.

Create Audio Snippets

We're starting to get a little more technical here. Fortunately, we live in the time of apps. In many cases, apps make repurposing your content so much easier. Audio is no exception. After recording your audio, you will generally edit it.

During your editing process, take the time to identify and isolate quotes or small snippets of the audio you feel best highlight what the full audio is about. Think of these snippets as very short movie trailers.

Once you identify these audio snippets, you can repurpose them in a few ways. For example, an isolated quote of twenty-four seconds or less can be uploaded to an app called Clammr. At the time of this writing, Clammr is an iOS only app. Think of it as the Twitter of the audio world. Once uploaded your snippet of audio, now called a Clammr, is available for listening to thousands of Clammr users.

As a bonus, you can also add brief descriptions and links as you post the file to the Clammr servers. Another cool thing about uploading to Clammr is that the Clammr app is one of the fourteen apps featured in Apple Carplay. Apple CarPlay is the interface on some cars that allows you to connect directly to your iPhone through a built-in touchscreen interface. This means that your audio snippets can be accessed through the touchscreen in your car instead of your phone. Pretty cool, eh?

If your audio is liked by other Clammr-ers, they can click on the provided links to go to the full version, which is usually in a podcast. If you've never heard of Clammr, I recommend checking it out. It's great way to find new content.

Create Audio Snippets for Other Platforms

What else can you do you with the audio snippets? Well, LinkedIn now allows you to add audio to your profile posts. The best part is that you don't have to change the content at all. You can take the snippet you uploaded to Clammr and post it directly to LinkedIn. The same piece of content is now used in two places.

Another app you can use for audio (which is still in its infancy as the time of this writing) is called Anchor. The Anchor app allows you upload or record directly into the app and post it. The interesting thing about this app is that it is not passive once posted, but instead becomes interactive.

With Clammr and other audio apps, once you post your content, that's pretty much it. It lives on that platform in its uploaded state until you pull it down. With Anchor, however, your content sits on the platform, but people who listen to it can add their comments to your original post. It's an interesting concept and one to keep an eye on for sure.

Create Audio from Your Presentations

Another way to create a piece of audio content is to record yourself while you are speaking or giving a group presentation. I like this method for a few reasons. It makes use of something you were already doing anyway. You were scheduled to give a presentation that requires you to talk, so why not record it?

When I do this, I use a lavalier microphone clipped to my jacket and hooked up to an old iPhone. I give my presentation as normal, capture the audio, and upload it to iTunes as a podcast.

As a bonus, you can easily go back and find those perfect snippets, separate them out and upload them to Clammr and the other platforms already mentioned.

Create a Podcast

I've saved the best for last! Creating a podcast is the ultimate goal for your audio content. I didn't start with podcasting because it can be very involved, especially if you want to release a quality show. Podcasts require quite a bit of planning, such as deciding on the type of show you want to produce: solo, interview-based, a combination of the two, storytelling, and the list goes on.

If you're interested in starting a podcast, here is a list of the basic things you will need:

- A computer
- A microphone (your computer mic won't cut it)
- Audio editing software (Audacity or Adobe Audition)
- An audio hosting company (Libsyn)
- A Real Simple Syndication (RSS) link provided by your hosting company
- Access to iTunes and/or Google Play

There is obviously a lot more involved when producing a podcast. If you are interested in learning more, you can listen to my podcast on how to create a podcast. The key takeaway in this section is understanding that you can upload your audio to a hosting service that will broadcast out your show on multiple channels.

Repurposing Your Video Content

By 2020, almost 80 percent of the content on the Web will be video-based. This means that, like it or not, if we want to stand out, we will need to get comfortable behind a camera. Video sits at the top of the Content Pyramid, because it can be technically challenging for you to create your content. It can also be very nerve-wracking, and as with audio, your production costs can start to get expensive depending on the quality of video you want to produce.

Create Written Content

The first way you can repurpose video is by having it transcribed into written content. You can do this using a service like the one discussed earlier, Rev.com. This will still cost you a dollar a minute to do. You can also do the same for free using YouTube's closed-captioning software. Once your video is uploaded, find the closed-captioning feature in your video manager and tell it to transcribe the video.

This service is free, but I will say that you get what you pay for. You will need to wordsmith yourself or use the polishmywriting.com site discussed earlier. Once your video is in written form, all of the written content repurposing items apply.

Create Audio Content

After recording yourself on video, it is very easy to "strip out" the audio from your file as long as you have the right software. I use a software program called Screenflow to do this.

Currently, Screenflow is only available for Macs. If you have a PC, Camtasia is the program for you. Once you have the audio file from your video, you can repurpose the audio in the ways described above, including creating a podcast.

Create a Screencast

If you use the software noted above, you can record yourself reading your slides or blog posts and capture your computer screen as a screencast at the same time. Once completed, you can upload it to YouTube. This might be a great way for many of you to break into the video content space, especially if you are not super comfortable in front of the camera. You can do the same with all of the written content you've produced. Just open up the software and start recording.

Video Record Your Podcast

Most podcasts are recorded audio only. This can be for several reasons: Your guest may be uncomfortable in front of the camera, you may be uncomfortable in front of the camera, you may not have the right software, and/or you may not have the bandwidth to handle video.

All of that aside, if you turn on the camera and record your podcast, you now have a video podcast. This means that you can pull out the audio and post it to your podcast hosting service of choice. Another approach is to use a service like Zoom. Zoom is free to use for up to two people, you and your guest. Zoom allows you to record your podcast using video. When you finish, Zoom automatically sends you a video file and an audio file—i.e., content in two mediums for distribution in two places.

Live Stream Video

This one is not going away, folks; live streaming is here to stay. There will be lots of entrants into the space over the next several years, and there will be many casualties as well. Just ask video pioneer Meerkat who closed up shop due to heavy competition from Twitter and Facebook Live.

Live streaming is not technically challenging, but it can be. In its simplest form, you open an app and push the Go Live button. Then there are users like Joel Comm, pioneers in the field who produce a very high-quality live video show. (If you've not heard of Joel, I recommend you check him out at http://joelcomm.com.) High-quality live streaming not only requires additional equipment and financial resources, it also requires a level of comfort in front of the camera few of us possess in the beginning.

The Beauty of the Content Pyramid

In case you hadn't realized, this is entire section on repurposing your content lives within the Content Pyramid. All content in the pyramid can be repurposed up or down the pyramid. As you move up the pyramid, so does the level of difficulty and cost required to produce high-quality content.

The beautiful thing about video—and the reason it is at the top of the pyramid—is that if you start with video, you can repurpose it relatively easily into all the other types of content.

To review, once you've recorded your video, you can strip out your voice to make audio content such as a podcast or isolated snippets for upload to Clammr or LinkedIn. Once your content is in the audio format, you can have it transcribed into written content using a service like Rev.com. Once you have written content, you can repurpose in any number of ways.

From now on, for every piece of content you produce, as you're creating it or reviewing it, consider the number of different ways you can reuse the same content. If you take a little time to plan in advance, you'll be able to expand your reach significantly with every piece of content you produce.

Exercise 17—Repurpose Your Content

For this exercise, you are going to repurpose the content you produced in Exercise 14. Use the Exercise 17 worksheet to complete this exercise. You can find it in the *CareerKred Workbook* at http://careerkredbook.com/workbook.

Reread your post. Look for quotes, snippets, and other ways you can turn your content into a new piece for a different platform. At a minimum, try to create the following three pieces of additional content:

- An Instagram quote post
- A Facebook post
- A Slideshare post

Doing this for one post will introduce you to new audiences and provide you with a much greater reach than you can achieve by only posting on your own website.

Create Step 3

Chapter 34

Content Curation

In addition to creating content during the Create step, you will also begin to curate content. Content curation is the process of collecting, organizing, and displaying (sharing) information on a topic or area of interest. In the Create step, this means sharing content created by others.

When giving a presentation, I like to ask the audience who they think is the largest content curator in the world. What do you think?

The two most common answers I get are museums and libraries. Both are great examples of content being collected, organized, and displayed by topic or area of interest. One involves things and the other, books.

While these two institutions do curate content, neither come close to matching the largest curator of information in the world: Google. Remember, Google's job is to collect, organize, and display information on topics or areas of interest.

Curation is what Google does. It's the job we trust it to do, to the tune of 3.5 billion times each and every day. Google also takes the added step to rank the results according to its proprietary algorithm. Because of this, we rely on Google to provide us with the best and latest information on anything we type in the search bar, and we trust the results. Why? Because we know that Google is constantly learning.

Every day Google's job is to discover new things, such as who the influencers are for any given topic. It indexes (curates) this new content and shares it via its search results. What does this have to do with you? Well, if you stop and think about it, you can be one of the influencers Google discovers.

You create great content. You're continually feeding your brain with information (curating) from people you look up to in your area of expertise, and you are sharing your information freely with others—in particular with those people who stop by and read your blog posts.

Now consider what happens when you start to share relevant information written by others. If you share it correctly, those people will take notice of you, and they may even begin to share *your* content with *their* audience. When this happens, your audience will begin to grow.

Why do you use Google? More pointedly, why don't you use Bing instead of Google? How about DuckDuckGo? Why not use DogPile? (Yes, DogPile is a real search engine.)

The answer is simple: You use Google because you know it. You like it, and you trust it. Know, like, and trust—all the ingredients needed for you to do business with Google.

But what if Google only returned results that it had created? If, instead of seeing articles from many sources, you only got the ones Google produced, would you still trust it? If Google did this, my guess is you would quickly find another source for your information. DogPile, here I come—who's with me?

We like and use Google for precisely this reason: It curates information from all types of sources so we don't have to.

When you produce content for your blog, the information naturally comes from you. It's your writing and your point of view. Your wiring may be influenced by information you have curated from others, but it is still your writing, and people will gravitate to you based on it. But what if, in addition to providing your thoughts and information, you were more like Google and provided information from other sources as well? Like Google, you're continually feeding your brain with information (curating) from people you look up to in your area of expertise. So why not share it with your audience as well?

Sharing information beyond what you create sends a signal to your audience that you know what you are talking about it because you are on top of what is happening in your niche. You know who the players are, and you really want your audience to be well-informed.

When you reach this point, you are performing a service that is essentially the same as the one Google provides. This is how you start to become recognized as a thought leader, an authority, the go-to person for your subject matter. Or as I like to say, you start to become the Google of your niche.

Become the Google of Your Niche

We've all come across people who we would consider to be the "Google of their niche." You recognize them quickly because, not only do they know and understand their topic inside and out, they can also refer you to others within the industry for additional information.

Think about the last person you came in contact with who was like this. Did you trust his or her opinion more, or less? Chances are you walked away from the conversation regarding the person to be, if not an expert, at the very least worthy of a referral to others.

Just this past week, I went to a sporting goods chain store looking for a pair of trail hiking shoes. I knew which shoes I wanted, thanks to Google, and I set about trying to find them. During my search, a nice young lady came up to me and asked if I needed any help.

I told her the brand and style of the shoe I was looking for, and she quickly responded, "I'm sorry, sir, but we're currently out of those shoes." This could have been the end of our conversation, but she quickly started telling me about some alternative brands sold in the store.

She was able to provide me with details about these shoes, including the advantages of one brand over the other. She even knew the foot type (i.e., pronated or not) that would work best with each shoe. Clearly, she knew her shoes. I was impressed, but I also really had my mind set on the shoes I had come into the store to find.

For the second time, she could have ended our conversation since they didn't have the shoes I was looking for. However, she recognized that I really wanted these shoes, so she did something most people in her position don't do. She told me which competitor sold the shoes I was looking for.

She explained that she regularly "shops" her competitors in order to determine which shoes they have in stock and the prices of those shoes—and she even picks up some new sales techniques along the way.

I was more than impressed. She even suggested that I hold off on my purchase for two days because the competitor was going to have a sale. Wow. I walked away from our conversation obviously impressed, but better yet, that store had just earned a loyal customer—for my next pair of shoes, anyway.

This is the power of curation. Sharing more than your own thoughts on your blog with others is a great way to position yourself as a thought leader and the go-to person in your niche.

Curate to Educate

To grow your CareerKred in your niche, you must learn as much of the pertinent information on your subject matter as you can. And despite what your sixteen-year-old child might tell you, it's not possible to learn *everything* on any given topic.

In order to "stay on top of your game," you need to be continually learning from those who have insights or experiences different from your own. After all, if you are not educating yourself by gaining the perspective of others, you are no longer growing personally or professionally. You become complacent, and you already know where that will get you.

Eventually this will impact your content because it will grow stale in the minds of your audience. When this happens, they will turn to someone else because they no longer hear any new perspectives from you.

That's why we start to curate content as a part of the Create step. It expands your thinking, helps keep your content fresh and relevant, and allows you to share the thoughts of others to further educate your audience.

Remember, this is the definition of the Relentless Giver. You are helping to educate others by sharing content from a wide variety of sources while at the same time using the opportunity to expand your reach and grow your brand.

Sharing Is Caring

"Sharing is caring," my son told me when he came home from his first day in kindergarten. Not only is this applicable on the kindergarten playground, it's very applicable when building your brand.

Sharing the content of others is counterintuitive initially for many of my clients. They believe that if they share the content of others, their audience will leave them and go to those other sources. This is an example of a scarcity mindset. This mindset is dangerous and will prevent you from ever reaching your full potential.

If you want to become known for something, you have to abandon the "he who has the knowledge has the power" mantra and adopt the "you can have everything in life you want if you will just help other people get what they want" mantra of Zig Ziglar.

Don't get me wrong—I do believe that having knowledge is powerful. In fact, knowledge is the key to unlocking your potential as you progress through the DICE process. However, I also believe there is far greater power in sharing your knowledge with others.

In fact, in today's sharing economy, sharing is expected. Tools like social media provide us with outlets to share the information we collect and organize with others who are interested in the topic. That's why content curation plays such a vital role in becoming a trusted source within your niche.

Become the Trusted Source within Your Niche

Take a minute and think of someone you go to for information on a topic—electronics, for instance. If you have a question about the latest electronic gadgets, this is the person you got to for answers. Did you think of someone? Why did is this particular person come to mind?

Is it because they are knowledgeable on the topic? Maybe they work in the industry. Maybe they are early adopters, or maybe they just really "geek out" about new technology. Odds are this person is all of the above. They are knowledgeable because they constantly keep up-to-date and share information by curating content from other brands and influencers in the industry. That's why you consider this person your go-to individual regarding questions about electronics.

This is why we curate. This is why we share what we know freely. This is key to building your brand, your CareerKred, and becoming the Google of your niche.

Chapter 35

Getting Started with Content Curation

Hopefully by now you understand the importance of curating content to build your brand. However, you might be thinking, *This sounds like a lot of work. How am I going to get this done?*

The good news is that there are several tools you can use to assist you with your content curation efforts. All of them depend on something we discussed a little earlier that may have seemed insignificant at the time but is critical to being found online and now for your curation efforts: keywords

Finding the Right Keywords

Like most things online, content curation relies heavily on keywords. Choosing the correct keywords means you'll curate content your audience will like. Choose the wrong ones, and you can very quickly go off-brand and confuse people.

In addition to choosing the "wrong" keywords, it's highly possible to select keywords that are either too high-level or too generic to actually make a difference in your online efforts. If you select a keyword that is too broad, for example—such as engineering or marketing manager—you won't be able to attract and engage an audience. You'll need to drill down a little further in order for your keywords to be effective.

To help you get started, let's walk through the steps you can take to identify the relevant keywords in your niche. I'm going to use the generic keyword *personal branding* to walk through the process of identifying thc right keywords for your niche.

Google Autocomplete

As you know, Google shifts through hundreds of thousands of websites in tenths of seconds to find relevant content for the keywords you are searching for on any given topic. The cool thing about this is that Google saves searches for future reference.

You may not realize it, but you've seen this every time you type something into the Google search bar. In fact, you've seen this happen so often that you probably take it for granted, but it's a very powerful way to identify potential keywords.

Have you noticed that as soon as you start to type into the search bar, Google automatically starts populating what it believes you want to search for? This is called autocomplete. It's a feature in Google's search algorithm designed to help you select what you are looking for by trying to predict the keyword you are typing.

Autocomplete is designed to speed up our interaction with Google. The algorithm "learns" each time new words are typed in the search box. In addition, the autocomplete algorithm will suggest alternative keywords to the one you are entering. This is where the magic happens with Google autocomplete.

To test this out, open up Google and type in one of the keywords you selected earlier. As you type, Google will populate the search bar with grayed out letters behind the cursor. This is autocomplete in action, trying to predict what you're going to type. Right below the search bar notice the number of results Google is predicting based on your keyword.

When I type in personal branding, for instance, Google suggests there are approximately 23 million possible results. This is why using broad keywords is not recommended. The category you're searching within contains too much information. In other words, many people are competing for that keyword. So if you want your content to rank in search results, you will need to go "deeper" into your niche and become more specific.

Before you click enter and after you've finished typing your complete keyword, pause just a moment and look at all of the keywords below the one in the search box that Google is suggesting you consider. Each one of these suggestions is a keyword someone else has searched for within Google.

The presented keywords are an example of what is called "niching down" or going deeper with your keyword. If you select one of these keywords instead of the one you typed, notice how the number of results change. Selecting "personal branding tips" instead of the broad term "personal branding," for example, yields only 6.8 million results versus 23 million results.

Selecting this "niched down" keyword acts to narrow down the competition. The deeper you go with your keywords, the better chance you have of showing up higher in search results.

Earlier I suggested that you use your first and last name for your domain. That way, when someone searches for you online, your name becomes a keyword. If your name is unique, you already have an advantage over someone with a more common name, say Joe Smith. (Sorry, Joe.)

Like Google autocomplete, adding your middle initial or a qualifier at the end of your name is how you are able to "niche down" in the category of Joe Smith. It not only serves as a way to differentiate you, but it allows Google to find you faster.

One more thing on autocomplete before we move on. Once you've finished typing your keyword, press the space bar. Notice that autocomplete provides you with different set of keywords, which allows you to niche down even further.

Another trick you can use after pressing the space bar is to enter a single letter—for instance, the letter "A." Google will now provide you with additional suggestions starting with the letter A after your keyword has been entered. This is where a qualifier word might come in handy. "Joe Smith actor or automotive," for example, will filter out many potential Google search results.

Google Suggestions

This is also a feature you probably have seen but not paid much attention to in the past. After you've typed in your keyword and pressed enter, once the results have been displayed, scroll all the way down to the bottom of the page.

At the very bottom, Google provides a small section title "Searches related to." All the clickable links are other related keywords to the one you entered, meaning people have searched for these keywords before. These are suggested as potential alternative keywords for you to use in order to go deeper into your topic. I recommend checking a few of them out, especially if you are in a competitive market.

Google Trends

Another useful tool Google provides for you to select keywords is Google Trends. Google Trends is based on Google Searches and shows how often a particular keyword is searched for relative to the total searches across various regions of the world and various languages.

As mentioned previously, since is Google is already keeping track of the keywords entered into its search bar, it's in a great position to show you how well or not so well any given keyword has performed over time. Entering your keyword into Google Trends will show you graphically how your keyword has trended over time and by geographical region.

From this you can discover the geographical area that is the most interested in the topic and whether or not your chosen keyword is trending up or down. Google Trends will also highlight related searches for your keyword. This is good because there are always smaller niches within the larger topic.

Google Trends is a great tool for making sure you don't attempt to rank for keywords people are no longer searching for.

Google Keyword Planner

Google's Keyword Planner tool is free to use; however, you will need an AdWords account to use it. You will not need to use the AdWords account except to gain access to the Keyword Planner. As you've probably already guessed, this method is a little more advanced—but so are the results.

This section is not meant to be a tutorial on AdWords. If you're interested in AdWords, search for it online; there is more than enough information out there to keep you busy for a long time. You can sign up for a free AdWords account and get access to the Keyword Planner tool at this link: https://adwords.google.com/home/tools/keyword-planner.

The Keyword Planner tool is complex and a little daunting at first. Fortunately, there are a number of classes you can take to teach you how to use it. It works much like a Google search, but you can enter one keyword, multiple keywords, or even website addresses into the Keyword Planner. Like a search result, Google will spit out a list of related keywords along with some simple metrics intended for you to gauge how "fierce" the competition is around each keyword. You'll even see how many searches Google gets for your keyword both locally and globally.

You can see historical statistics and information on a suggested new list of keywords Google created based on your keyword by multiplying several lists of keywords together. This tool is not for the faint of heart. It is complicated, but it will also yield more advanced results. Give it a shot and see what you think.

Other Places to Find Keywords

There are many places online where you can "vet out" potential keywords, but none of them can tell you exactly which ones you should use. As you continue to create and curate content, you'll start to see which keywords resonate with your audience. Finding the right keyword is a constant refinement process.

Others places to look for keywords include the following:

- Keywordtool.io—You can find up to fifty alternative keywords for free.
- Amazon—Amazon uses an autocomplete algorithm as well, with the bonus that what people are looking for is usually something they want to purchase.
- LinkedIn—Correct, LinkedIn uses an autocomplete feature as well. You'll be able to find people, groups, and companies who use your keywords.

You can put as much or as little time into finding the keywords you want people to know you for. I recommend putting in the time to understand which keywords you should use because it's that important for getting found online.

Exercise 18—Capture Your Keywords

In this exercise, you're going to take the keywords you identified earlier and narrow them down to the ones you want to use going forward. You can use any of the methods described above.

Use the Exercise 15 worksheet to document this exercise. You can find it in the *CareerKred Workbook* at http://careerkredbook.com/workbook.

For each of your current keywords, find three to five alternative keywords. Conduct searches for those keywords, and then review the articles found in the search results. Make note of the person writing the articles and whether or not the search results are relevant to your area of expertise. Just because Google suggested it, doesn't mean it's correct.

Capture all of the "new" alternative keywords along with your current ones. You're going to need them going into the next section.

Chapter 36

Tools for Content Curation

When done correctly, the time you commit to curate content doesn't have to equal hours. If it did, I wouldn't recommend that you do it. In order to be able to effectively "comb" through the content of others in an efficient manner, you will need to make use of a few online tools.

Using these tools will save you time and allow you to scale your curation efforts. When I started curating content, I focused only on a few people who were creating great content in my area of expertise that I wanted to make a connection with. I recommend that you do the same.

As you'll learn in the engage step, it not only makes it easier to keep up with, but it will allow you to form a deeper relationship with these individuals. Forming relationships with people you would not otherwise be able to meet is another key reason to do content curation. Remember, as a Relentless Giver, you are serving others while at the same time advancing your cause.

What follows is a list of the tools I use to curate content as well as some of the basics on what to look for in curated content and how to share it with your audience.

BuzzSumo

Despite its quirky name, BuzzSumo is a great tool for tracking content on all social networking sites and ranking them based on the number of shares on Facebook, Twitter, LinkedIn, Google+, and Pinterest. With your keywords selected, you can use BuzzSumo to analyze all types of content, and it can help you find the key influencers in your area of expertise.

You can also use BuzzSumo to see what your competitors are doing with content for the keywords you've selected. BuzzSumo can even help you decide which social media networks you should consider using.

To get started, all you need to do is go to BuzzSumo.com. Type your keyword in the search bar and hit enter. BuzzSumo does the rest.

From the results, you'll be able to see the most shared content for your keywords. You'll get the title of the article and the author. In addition, you get to see on which social networks the article was shared the most.

To summarize, use BuzzSumo to determine the following.

- Influencers in your areas of expertise
- Articles about your area of expertise
- Keywords your competitors are using
- The social network you should consider for your posts

RSS Readers

The next essential ingredient in content curation is an RSS reader. RSS (Rich Site Summary), also called Really Simple Syndication, utilizes standard Web feed formats to publish frequently updated information such as blog entries, news headlines, audio, and video.

These RSS feeds enable publishers to syndicate data automatically. This means that if you subscribe to the RSS feed of an influencer in your niche, you will receive an update every time that person publishes a new post.

An RSS reader allows you to collect various feeds from all over the Internet into one convenient location. It very much acts as the newspaper that used to be delivered to your front porch. The latest news and blog posts from your area of expertise are delivered directly to your device of choice each and every day.

Although I've used RSS readers for while, it was my conversation with Todd Lohenry that convinced me of the importance of RSS readers, especially when it comes to collecting and curating information.

There are many different RSS readers available. There is no "right one" to use. The only right one is the one that works for you. Here are a couple to consider.

Feedly

For years my RSS reader of choice was Feedly. Feedly is a Web-based tool that provides a pretty powerful way to organize, read, and share the content of your favorite sites. It's like Google for content specifically related to your area of expertise.

Feedly features different layout options, allowing you to mark articles as read as well as tag and share articles right from the application. Feedly is a great RSS reader for you to start with. It integrates with other tools that can be used to create chains of simple conditional statements, which we'll cover in a minute. As a bonus, you can get started for free.

Once you're logged in, you simply provide Feedly with the URL of the website you want to follow, and Feedly takes care of the rest. After you've added a few sites to follow into Feedly, your dashboard will start to resemble a digital newspaper.

Inoreader

Another good RSS reader option is Inoreader. Despite having used Feedly for many years, based on a recommendation from Todd Lohenry, I started using Inoreader. And yes, in case you were wondering, at first it felt like I was cheating on Feedly.

Functionally, Inoreader does the same work as Feedly but with a different user interface.

RSS tools like Inoreader and Feedly for content curation provide three benefits. First, you stay up-to-date on what is happening in your area of expertise. This keeps your mind filled with fresh ideas and keeps your idea muscle working.

Second, you save time because you no longer need to visit your favorite sites daily looking for new and useful information. Any new information comes directly to you.

Third, because the information comes directly to you, you can decide what information is worthy to share with your audience. Another advantage, as I touched on before, is that they both integrate with other online tools used to create chains of simple conditional statements that allow you to share information automatically.

Applets

An applet is any small application that performs one specific task. It runs within the scope of a dedicated widget or a larger program, often as a plug-in, and is designed to be placed on a Web page.

Technical mumbo jumbo, I know. While applets can be used for many different things, the beauty is not only their simplicity but how they can be leveraged to amplify your content curation efforts.

Don't worry, there is no coding required in order to use applets. If there were, I would not be talking about them in this book. Fortunately for both of us, there are Web applications that take care of the coding for us. What we get to do is take advantage of this programming by using tools like IFTTT.com and Zapier.com.

IFTTT.com

IFTTT is a free Web-based service that allows you to create chains of simple conditional statements that are triggered based on changes to other Web services such as Gmail, Facebook, Instagram, and Pinterest. IFTTT is an abbreviation that stands for "If This Then That."

What I love about this tool is that it works exactly like the name of the software implies. "If this" happens, "then" do "that." For example, if a new blog post appears on your favorite website, then you want that post to appear on your RSS reader.

I know this may sound complicated, but IFTTT has made the user interface as simple as selecting boxes. You simply tell the software you want to make a new conditional statement, and then you tell click on boxes with your desired icons to create the statement.

The only real limitations to these conditional statement programs are the other Web services they integrate with. It's highly possible that you'll need to use two services to specific integrations.

Zapier.com

Zapier does exactly the same thing as IFTTT—it allows you to connect apps you use every day to automate tasks and save time. I use both IFTTT and Zapier.

With Zapier, you build what are called Zaps. Your Zaps are then used to automate tasks you want to do over and over. Think of a Zap as a blueprint. It functions the same way as IFTTT, in that you tell it which Web services to connect to and what specific actions that connection should drive.

Building a Zap is as easy as building a condition in IFTTT. The only real difference between these two Web services is the integrations they offer. That's why, for your curation efforts, you may need to use both.

Social Media "Go-Betweens"

There is no such thing as a "social media go-between." I made up this term to illustrate the fact that, as you gain confidence in your ability to curate content, you'll want to start using tools that serve as a "go-between" from your RSS reader to your published content.

These platforms allow you to schedule content to release on specific dates at specific times. You can also review, edit, and delete content before it gets posted online in your name. We'll talk more specifically about how to use these tools in the Engage step, but for now know that these "go-betweens" really do serve as a buffer between you and your audience.

My favorite go-between is called Buffer—I'm a huge fan. I love everything about the tool. The interface is intuitive, and it's simple to use. Buffer serves as a go-between and allows you to review, edit, delete, and schedule content.

With the click of your mouse, you can post content to multiple social media accounts. Using a tool like Buffer helps get your name "out there" faster and allows you to "be everywhere" with very little effort.

The Create Step Checklist

- ☐ Take the Digital Brand Assessment (if not already completed)
- ☐ Score: ______________

Step #1 - Content

- ☐ Complete the Content Muscle worksheet
- ☐ Select and write one article from your Content Muscle worksheet

Step #2 - Repurpose Your Content

- ☐ Complete the Repurpose Your Time worksheet
- ☐ Repurpose the content you created in step one, into three pieces of content

Step #3 - Content Curation

- ☐ Identify and narrow down the keywords you want to be known for
- ☐ Identify influencers and industry sites to follow
- ☐ Setup content curation accounts:
    - ☐ Setup RSS Reader account (Feedly or Inoreader)
    - ☐ Setup your Applet account (IFTTT.com or zapier.com)
    - ☐ Setup your Go-Between account (Buffer)

Part Six

The Engage Step

"The only people with power today are the audience, and you ignore that at your peril." —Simon Cowell

Use the power of social media to amplify your digital brand and reputation.

Digital Brand Assessment Score: 76–100

Congratulations! You are in the top 3 percent of all assessment takers. You are found in searches, and you create and publish content in alignment with your brand regularly. You are here because of good old-fashioned hard work.

At this point, you are getting recognized, and you've earned the "right" to go off-brand from time to time. Your audience will not penalize you for it; in fact, they may even be drawn closer to you because of it. Speaking of your audience, you've noticed that you've earned a growing one. The key now is make sure you are nurturing your audience through both your actions and your content.

Here are some common thoughts for people who find themselves with a score in this range.

1. I want to be a credible and trusted advisor.
2. I want to continue to grow my network.
3. I want to use social media to grow and interact with my audience.
4. I want to be "everywhere" online.
5. I want to use my brand to attract clients and referrals.

The Engage step is all about getting the word out about you and your services. It's about embracing the Relentless Giver mindset and using it every day to teach everything you know.

Chapter 37

Get Engaged

The last step in the DICE process, Engage, is the most important when it comes to building trust and credibility in your field. It is the culmination of all your work to this point.

Over the last few sections of this book, you've walked through discovering your brand and strategically integrating it online. We've also discussed the importance of creating content and how it helps to demonstrate your expertise.

If you were to stop here and go no further with the DICE process, you would be in a much better place than the vast majority of your competition. You would get found when they are not, and you would be recognized for your CareerKred while they are not.

By all accounts, that's a pretty good spot to be in. But if you really want to amplify your CareerKred, your reputation, and your brand, you must get involved directly with your audience in order to establish a meaningful connection. In other words, if you want to continue to build trust with your audience, you need to engage with them.

Ways to Engage

There are many different ways you can engage with your audience:

1. Networking
2. Social Media
3. Twitter chats
4. Like and commenting

5. Public speaking
6. eMail newsletters
7. Curating content
8. Attending conferences
9. Surveys
10. Phone calls (Yes, actually speaking to people)
11. Answering emails
12. Streaming video
13. Webinars

This is not an exhaustive list; there are many other ways you can engage with your audience, but this list should give you an idea of what the Engage step is all about.

To this point, much of the DICE Process can be done from behind a computer. And while some of the actions in the list above can be done via a computer as well, some of these actions require you to get out into the wild, so to speak, and leave the computer behind.

However, regardless of whether the actions are in front of or behind a computer, they all have one thing in common: All of them require you to engage, to participate, to attract, to involve your audience in a more personal and meaningful conversation.

The Engage step is intertwined with the Create step. With every post you make, you have the possibility for engagement. Every time you curate someone else's content, you have the possibility for engagement.

For you to continue to build trust, you can't let these opportunities pass you by.

Unlike the other steps in the DICE process, the Engage step has a plethora of actions you can take, and you are essentially free to choose your preferred method for engaging your audience. However, there are two actions you should take regardless of the others you select: Networking and Social Media.

Engage Step 1

Chapter 38

Network Like a Rock Star

David J. P. Fisher, author of the *Networking in the 21st Century* series of books, pushed me over the edge and finally helped me understanding the importance of networking. I know that for some of you, hearing the word *networking* is like fingernails running down a chalkboard. You hate it. I wouldn't be surprised if you're tempted to skip this section all together.

I understand this feeling. I've been there. I hated networking, too, but here's my promise to you. By the time you've finished reading this section, you will feel very differently about networking. I'm not saying you're going to want to rush out and start meeting new people straightaway, but I am saying you will gain a new appreciation for what networking really is and why you need to be doing it. Every. Single. Day.

If you get anxious or uptight at the mention of the word networking, it's likely that at some point in your life, personally or professionally, you attended some networking "event" that sucked the life out of you.

If this describes a situation you were in, then the chances are high that you would agree wholeheartedly with Don Orlando, who defines traditional networking as "a mutually mortifying ritual whereby we impose on every friend, relative, and stranger to ask for something they cannot give us, which is usually a job."

Hannah Morgan agrees. "When we reach out to somebody and immediately say, 'I'm looking for a job. Can you take a look at my resume,' we automatically shut the door on that opportunity versus showing some interest in the person."

Networking has gotten a bad rap for this very reason—people going in for the ask (remember the Askholes?) without showing any interest in you personally. And while I agree that this may have been your experience in the past, the simple truth is that, if you want to become known in your niche as an expert, you need to network. It's inevitable. In fact, it's required.

Knowing this, its time to set aside any preconceived notions you may have about networking and decide to give it another chance. However, this time, you are going to approach it as a Relentless Giver.

To be successful at networking, you need to have the right mindset because, as David told me, "If you really think about it, networking facilitates life."

A New Way to Think about Networking

As David and I discussed the ins and out of networking in the twenty-first century, it became clear to me that he believes that we all live in a network. In fact, he said almost those exact words. The thing is, though, chances are good that you don't consider your life to be a series of networks.

David challenges you to consider the following. "Every time you talk to friends, coworkers, or you're just interacting socially in the world, you're networking." This statement was the key turning point for me.

You see, my family and I recently moved to the state of Colorado. When we moved here, we essentially knew no one. My children knew no one. I did know a few people through work, but I didn't know things such as the best area to live, despite having traveled here many times throughout the years for work.

So when we arrived, I started asking people questions: Where is the best Mexican restaurant? Who do you recommend for a doctor? Which is the best high school? These seem like innocent questions, but what they really were, when taken in total, was the beginning of a new network for my family and myself. As David said, I was using networking to facilitate life. I think David helps to put this in perspective with his definition of networking:

> Networking is a web of relationships with other people with the purpose of finding mutual support and business solutions.

"A web of relationships with the purpose of mutual support"—this definition screams Relentless Giver.

Here's another way for you to think about networking. Answer this question: How did you meet your significant other?

Personally, my wife and I met because we were introduced by a coworker. That coworker was part of my network. Maybe you were introduced to your significant other while attending a party thrown by a friend. Said friend introduced you to someone in his or her network who in turn introduced you to your significant other.

That's how networking facilitates life.

Networking Is a Skill

Another reason people don't like networking is because they feel it is something reserved for salespeople or people who are more outgoing. You would probably classify them as extroverts. You may even believe these same people were "born" with the ability to network. It's in their "blood," so to speak.

Richard Kirby, career coach and author of the book *Fast Track Your Job Search*, introduced the following concept to me: Networking is a skill. When I first heard him say this, I had to ask him to repeat it. *Networking is a skill.*

Take minute to really consider that statement. If networking is indeed a skill, just as any of the skills you identified way back in Exercise 2, networking can be learned. You can learn to become a better networker.

Now before you hit me with the introvert/extrovert argument, consider this. If you believe networking is a skill, then the label you place on yourself doesn't matter. Anyone, introverts and extroverts alike, can learn it.

Merging this concept with the previous one, networking facilitates life, and you can easily see that each day you are learning and improving your networking skills. With every conversation and with every question you ask, you are building your networking muscle.

Networking = Relationships

Another key concept about networking is that it's about building relationships. Thinking back to David's definition of networking, it's a web of relationships. In order words, "networking is not transactional, it's relational," and those relationships, like newly planted seeds, need time to grow.

Odds are, when you think about networking, your first thought is about that "one person" who approached you as if the meeting was a transaction. Rather than making your meeting about finding something that is of interest for both of you, they made it about them.

This person took zero time to think about you and your needs, and a result you walked away unimpressed, maybe even a bit miffed. That's why, according to Hannah Morgan, "You've got to work and build relationships. It's not a slamdunk. It's not a one hit wonder. This all takes some time."

Good networking, in addition to facilitating a life, is a skill that can be learned. It requires time to learn how to do it properly, and it also requires time to build relationships. Have you ever heard the expression "Build your network before you need it"? This is exactly why.

You may be wondering at this point: *If networking is so important, with whom should I be networking?* Good question. Let's talk about that.

Weak Connections

There are two types of people you will want to include in your network: 1) strong connections, the people you see and interact with frequently, and 2) weak connections, the people you see every once in awhile. Of course in our digital-first world, the word *see* can mean both online and offline.

Why does this matter? Well, during my discussion with David, he mentioned that "most of the opportunities we get do not come from the people we know well," meaning that our strong connections typically come from what he called our weak connections.

Weak connections include the people we know, either personally or digitally, who may be in different areas of expertise and have a different information and knowledge base than we do.

The reason these weak connections are so important to our networks is that, as David put it, "the people we see all of the time, know the same stuff that we know." These weak connections operate outside our sphere of influence and offer us a diversity of information and perspectives we can't get from our strong connections.

When it comes to our careers, Hannah Morgan believes it's a great career move to spend time with our weak connections. "Let's not hang with the same people all the time. We need to have diversity in our professional life and in our personal life."

Another benefit that comes from our weak connections is that they know people we do not. This is where the opportunities come from. Every time we interact with someone online, at a conference, at a meet up, or at a dreaded networking event, even though it may not seem like it at the time, that person has the potential to become a weak connection for us.

The next time you casually meet someone at a party, a dinner, a conference, or a networking event, pay attention to his or her story. Don't treat the meeting as transactional. Instead, look at it as an opportunity to learn more about the person and how you might be able to help that individual. You never know where your weak connection may take you.

A Connection Strategy

Depending on which report you read, as many as 80 percent of jobs today are unadvertised. If eight out of ten jobs are unadvertised, how are they ever filled? The answer is networking.

However, in order for your networking efforts to work, you need a connection strategy. In fact, if you don't like the term *networking*, then use the phrase *connection strategy* instead. A connection strategy is exactly what it sounds like: a strategy you develop and execute on that will serve to grow your connections—i.e., your network.

Sound daunting? Well, it isn't once you know how. A good connection strategy consists of three parts: defining your goals, identifying people to connect with, and knowing where those people hang out.

Your Networking Goals

A good connection strategy starts by answering two questions:

1. What do you want to be known for?
2. What are you trying to do in your professional life?

It may seem weird to start a connection strategy by defining your goals, but as the Cheshire Cat said, "If you don't know where you're going, then any path will take you there."

You need to identify where you want to go professionally. A common challenge with many of my clients is that they cannot articulate where they want to go professionally. The good news is that, by defining your brand early on, you should have a really good handle on answering these two questions.

Who Should You Connect With?

Once you've defined your goals, you need to start thinking about who you want to connect with and why. Remember, you're building a relationship, not a follower count. Your reason for connecting with someone can be as simple as you look up to the person or as "complex" as he or she is a hiring manager.

As a Relentless Giver, your goal with every connection should be to help that person in some way. Add a little value to his or her life, so to speak. Understanding why you want to connect with someone and how you can help him or her is the starting point for building your connection strategy.

Building your connection strategy is not rocket science, nor does it need to be time consuming. To get started, open up your favorite spreadsheet software and label the first column "Name." Make a list of people you know to be influencers in your area of expertise.

Next to the Name column, add a column labeled "Why" and one next to it labeled "How I help." Complete the rows for ten people in your industry. If you can't come up with ten names, then do twenty, as Claudia Altucher would tell you to do.

Once you have ten names of people in your area of expertise, list another ten names of people you would like to know who are not in your niche. Just so we're clear, I'm not talking about Dwayne Johnson or Lady Gaga. I'm talking about others who are influential in their own niche that happens to be a little tangential to your own. In other words, your weak connections.

Hannah Morgan emphasizes the importance of reaching out beyond your area of expertise and into your weak connections. "We don't need to be playing in the same sandbox to benefit from knowing one another. It's being able to learn from other people, because we can learn from everybody, and the perspectives of somebody not in your field could be very beneficial to you in the long run."

Where Do Your People Hang Out?

Generally speaking, you're going to connect with people via email. However, you can also make connections with them in other places as well—for example, where they hang out both off-line and online. This is important, because it makes no sense for you to go to a local chamber of commerce meeting or other networking event if your connections don't go there.

Back on your spreadsheet, after the "How I Help" column, add one more column called "Where." In this column, list the different places you can find your connections—places such as their social media accounts and usernames or handles and the meet ups or conferences they attend. The more you can find out, the better.

With your connection strategy in place, begin reaching out to the people on your spreadsheet. Be sincere and authentic, and remember you are a Relentless Giver, so look for those areas of commonalities and use them as your "in."

Don't underestimate the power of social media in your connection strategy. PR warrior Trevor Young views social media as a mindset that "allows you to distribute your content and drive conversations around the things you want to be known for."

This is why finding potential connections on Twitter and LinkedIn who share your mindset is so important. Articles they've written and published online can provide you with what you need to leverage the power of content curation.

Exercise 19—Your Connection Strategy

In this exercise, you're going to develop your connection strategy. Use the Exercise 19 worksheet to document this exercise. You can find it in the *CareerKred Workbook* at http://careerkredbook.com/workbook.

There are three steps to complete this exercise:

1. Defining your goals
2. Identifying people to connect with
3. Knowing where those people hang out

Using the steps and tools already identified, take the time to determine the individuals you want to connect with. Remember, these should be people who you look up to in your area of expertise, people who are regularly publishing content, and people you find interesting.

Chapter 39

Content Curation for Networking

In the Create step, we discussed the reasons behind content curation. I also shared some tools you can you use to get your content curation efforts started. If you've begun using those tools, by now you've discovered that content curation can be time consuming. But it doesn't have to be.

In this section, I'm going to cover the "recipe" I use to amplify my content curation. But I don't just do it for the sake of doing it; I amplify my content curation efforts for the purpose of expanding my network, specifically my weak connections. It all starts by finding the right people.

Finding People on Social Media

If you're going to expand your network and boost your CareerKred, initially you need to focus your content curation efforts on individuals within your niche. I find individuals in my niche using the following methods:

1. BuzzSumo
2. LinkedIn
3. Authors

BuzzSumo and LinkedIn both serve similar functions for your content curation efforts. Both allow you to search using your keywords. BuzzSumo will show you individuals who have published articles already, and these will be the key people you will target in your curation efforts.

LinkedIn requires a little more work. It will show you individuals who have your keywords in their profile, but they may not necessarily be posting content. In order for your curation efforts to work, the individuals you want to network with need to be posting content.

Authors are easier, for obvious reasons. If they have written a book, chances are very high they will also be posting content online. Writers tend to write.

In all cases, regardless of which source the individual comes from, capture his or her name and immediately head to Twitter. Once there, read that person's bio and click on the link back to his or her homepage. When you're on the website, check for a blog. If the person has one—and nearly everyone who has their own website does—make a note and move to the next step.

Use Your RSS Reader

The next step is to head over to your RSS reader of choice (in my case, Inoreader). You can do the same thing I'm going to describe in Feedly or any other RSS reader. Using your keywords, take a few minutes to create a folder for each one. In many cases you can "lump" together a few keywords into one folder, or topic. The point here is to not have twenty folders to manage. I use four main folders.

1. Personal Branding
2. Online Reputation Management
3. Career-Related
4. Podcast Guests

Could you create one folder for everything? Yes, but I don't recommend it. Keeping them segregated by topic will help you keep straight in your mind why you selected that individual or website in the first place.

A quick note here: You don't have to follow only individual's websites. There are many websites out there that are based around a specific topic. These sites make use of a variety of authors in order to keep their content fresh and their feeds full. Talk about a goldmine of potential weak connections.

As an example, for my Career-related folder, I track the RSS feed for themuse.com and careeraddict.com. It's a great way to find new insights, authors, and potential influencers.

Once you've created your folders, enter the website of the person you want to follow into the search function of your RSS reader or, as Hannah told us earlier, strategically stalk that site. Once the reader returns the RSS feed, add it to the appropriate folder.

Do this for every individual or website you want to keep tabs on. This accomplishes two things for you. First, it enables you to quickly scan every day any new articles that were posted so you can keep up-to-date on the latest goings on in your niche. Second, it gets you ready for the next step in supercharging your content curation.

IfThisTenThat (IFTTT.com)

Now that you have your RSS reader populating with content for the websites you want to follow, you need to use this content to drive your curation efforts. However, posting each new article to your social media channels one by one is a huge pain, so you're not going to do that.

I mentioned two applets earlier, IFTTT.com and Zapier.com. They both offer the same thing, but my personal favorite is IFTTT. You can automatically post your curated content in two ways: directly to your social media feed or to what I referred to earlier as a go-between.

I do not recommend posting directly to your social media accounts. Before you post anything, you should review it to ensure it is congruent with the message you want to send and aligned with what you want to be known for. This is a little less important when posting from an individual's site, but when posting from a topic-based site, it can be very easy to go off-brand. This is why I recommend using IFTTT to send content to a go-between.

Once you've set up an account, IFTTT will ask you to create your first recipe. This is a guided process that will take you no more than six steps that can be completed in under a minute. Click the button that says New Applet. You will see the phrase If This Then That appear in the middle of your screen. The word THIS will be in a different color, usually blue. Click it.

You will now be able to choose a service—your recipe, as it's called. In this case, you'll select your RSS reader first. Once you've chosen your RSS reader, you'll be provided with a list of services, called triggers, to choose from. A trigger is a specific action that drives another action—classic cause and effect.

In this case, select the trigger "New Article in Folder." Selecting this will take you to the next step, where you'll choose which folder the desired action should come from. In my case I would select my Personal Branding folder, which tells IFTTT to note when a new article is found there.

After selecting the desired folder, once again If This Then That will fill your screen. This time the word THAT will be highlighted in blue. Click it. Now you will select the application in which "that" action will occur. For our purposes, you will select Buffer.

Quick note: You will need to create a Buffer account (don't worry, it's free!) in order to continue the process. Also, the first time you use any apps integrated with IFTTT, you will need to confirm this is OK.

When the Buffer triggers come up, select Add to Buffer. Your next screen (step five of six) allows you to either add an ingredient or simply create the action. Adding an ingredient lets you customize the content that is populated in your action. In the beginning I recommend going with the default, so click the Create action button.

The final step is verifying that the action you just set up is correct. Take a moment to read the If This Then That statement you just created. In my example, it reads "If new article in folder Personal Branding on Inoreader, then add to Twitter Buffer RyanRhoten." If you agree with your statement, click Finish, and you're ready for the last and final step to automatically curating your content.

Buffer

Earlier I referred to Buffer as a social media go-between. It fits into your process between the content creator and your audience. Buffer is mainly a social posting scheduler for social media. It works perfectly for Twitter, but at the time of this writing, it also works with Facebook (profiles and pages), LinkedIn (profiles and pages), Google+, Pinterest, and Instagram.

Buffer gives you total control over your posting schedule without having to schedule every single post separately, and it makes it super easy to share any page you're reading or have recently finished reading. It also schedules posts from IFTTT.com.

When your applet is triggered by IFTTT, it automatically moves the new content into Buffer, where it is formatted and placed in a queue. As a free user you can queue up ten posts.

Every morning and a few times throughout the day, I open up my Buffer app and review the content that has accumulated. My review process looks something like this:

1. I review the title. Is it intriguing? Does it seem like something my audience would benefit from?
2. If I'm not sure, I click the link in the post so I can review the article.
3. Based on my review, I determine if it's a good fit.
4. If it's not a good fit, I delete the content from the queue.
5. If it is a good fit, I take note of the author's name.
6. I head over to Twitter and find the author's Twitter handle.
7. I add the Twitter handle to the posted content.
8. I add a comment (the length depends on characters available).
9. I let the content post as scheduled.

Being able to review and personalize the content before it's posted to social media is awesome. It makes the content look more professional, and by adding a comment you are more likely to capture the author's attention.

A word of caution, though. The recipe I've just described is both a blessing and a curse. The blessing should be obvious, but the curse is born from the blessing. You see, once you set up this recipe, it will run. It will run all day, every day, unless you stop it. Therefore, if you have a chosen a website based on a topic that uses many different authors, your queue will fill up very fast. But that's not the problem. Since the topic-based website employs many authors, there's a chance that some of the content in your queue will not be 100 percent appropriate for your audience.

This is why I check my queue every morning and then several times throughout the day. But even with this level of attentiveness, a few off-brand tweets or posts will escape my viewing. This is not a brand-killer, but it is something you should be aware of as you step up your efforts to engage with your audience via social media.

Engage Step 2

Chapter 40

Using Social Media

We've established that one of the best ways today to engage your audience as well as expand your network is through social media. As soon as I say that to my coaching clients, the very next words out of their mouths are usually, "Yes, but which one?"

Since there are so many social media platforms out there for you to choose from, it's easy to see why it can be confusing. Such an abundance of platforms leads to the biggest mistakes I see business professionals making when building their CareerKred. Without a clear understanding of which platforms can best help you boost your CareerKred, you'll probably end up choosing them all.

Think back to the Google search you conducted in Exercise 8. Did you discover a graveyard of old social media profiles—profiles you created on what was at the time the latest and greatest social media platform? You know you did. We've all done it.

And therein lies a fundamental problem most of us have when it comes to social media. We believe that in order to get our names out there quickly (not correctly, mind you) and get found faster, we need to be on every social media platform that comes out.

This mindset is reiterated by many people online who tout the mantra "Be everywhere." While I agree that the more places you can be found will help you establish your CareerKred faster, when getting started, being everywhere will only serve to burn you out.

For my coaching clients, I recommend using no more than two or three platforms at first. Your goal with them is simple: You want to become really, really good at using them. This approach will minimize your level of overwhelm and aligns with Todd Lohenry's thought process: "You don't need to master seventeen different social networks at the same time. It's possible to start simple and stay simple. You stand a much better chance of getting found."

Start simple and stay simple. Our world is too complex as it is.

By narrowing your focus to a few vital platforms initially, you will help people find you faster. You will also reduce your workload and increase the chances that you will stay in engaged. Trying to manage multiple platforms is a great way to burn out quickly.

Social Media Is All about Relationships

Expanding your network used to mean attending those icky networking events. If you wanted to build meaningful relationships, face-to-face was the way to do it, and you had to go. It didn't matter whether you considered yourself an introvert or an extrovert, these events felt forced on you rather than something you wanted to do.

That's what's so great about social media. Whether you hate networking or not, social media levels the playing field for us all. It allows you to connect with people you don't know in a meaningful way without needing to subject yourself to an hour of those mutually mortifying rituals.

But all the social media tools available today won't help you if you don't choose the right ones and use them correctly. That's why I recommend adopting two key mindsets as you approach networking via social media:

1. Be a Relentless Giver.
2. Don't be an Askhole.

We've covered the Relentless Giver thoroughly, so I won't belabor it any further; however, thinking about social media as a conversation, not a conversion, is critical to your success.

Don't Be an Askhole

One of the biggest problems people experience with social media are the ask-first people. Earlier I referred to these people as Askholes, and I don't think there is a more fitting term for them.

As much good as social media can bring us, unfortunately it is also an enabler for bad behaviors. This is where Askholes come into play. Trevor Young would remind us that "social media isn't changing who we are." These same bad actors who don't have any filters off-line essentially means that when they sit in front of a keyboard, they are not going to have any filters there either.

Hannah Morgan, A.KA. the Career Sherpa, believes people become Askholes because "they're eager for the result." So rather than have a conversation with you, they immediately go for the conversion. It's the wrong way to go.

Instead, you must see that social media is *conversation*, not a conversion.

Not being an Askhole on social should be a no-brainer, but as the Darwin Awards prove every year, there's really no such thing as a no-brainer. Therefore, take the time when you get on social media to focus on a couple of platforms. Use them to build relationships and have conversations with interesting people.

Don't rush to the result because you never know where an honest conversation might lead you. Once you adopt the mindsets above, you will find networking via social media much more enjoyable—dare I say even fun?

When meeting someone new online for the first time, always ask yourself how you can help this person. Look for ways to build a relationship with them rather than just adding another number to your follower count.

With all of this in mind and your mindset in check, you still need to know which platforms to focus your time and energy on. As a business professional, I recommend that you start building your CareerKred using two platforms: Twitter and LinkedIn.

Chapter 41

Twitter Chats

I believe that Twitter chats are the easiest, fastest, and quickest way for you to demonstrate your expertise on social media.

A twitter chat allows you to be a Relentless Giver.

Mark Babbitt (@MarkSBabbitt) refers to Twitter chats as "keyboard nicotine," and rightfully so. I don't remember now how I found out about them, but once I discovered them, I was hooked. Maybe it was the nicotine.

Madalyn Sklar (@MadalynSklar) in her Twitter Chat Playbook online course says, "Twitter chats are a great way to boost your brand awareness while engaging with your audience."

What Is a Twitter Chat?

A Twitter chat is a sixty-minute conversation held on Twitter. The conversation usually revolves around a specific topic—personal branding, for example—and a predetermined hashtag. (More on hashtags soon.)

Personal branding expert Maria Elena Duron (@mariaduron) facilitates one of the longest-running Twitter chats, #Brandchat. Over the years she has built a very loyal tribe of like-minded individuals. She refers to the #Brandchat participants as "Branditoes," and while she is the host, she knows who the real experts are on the Twitter chat:

> To me the Branditoes are the experts. When they come to the chat, we have a room full of experts, just as you do in a mastermind group where

one person isn't more of an expert than anyone else; everybody is sharing the best that they can share in the time together.

"Like-minded people who form a mastermind group"—until Maria said it, I'd never looked at Twitter chats that way. But when you stop to think about it, Twitter chats are a great place to learn more about a specific topic, as well as find other like-minded people who can help you with a particular challenge, similar to the environment in a mastermind group.

Mark Babbitt views Twitter chats as a method of "peer-to-peer mentoring on steroids." Twitter chats are all about being the Relentless Giver. For one hour, you surround yourself with like-minded individuals in a mastermind-type format for the purpose of learning from and educating others. During that hour, participants freely share their best information with each other. In my opinion, you can't find another place online where peer-to-peer mentoring is as powerful.

Getting Started

OK, you're convinced and ready to participate. The good news is that participating in a Twitter chat is not difficult; however, it can be a bit confusing the first time you show up. Let's walk through how to get started.

You only need two things to participate in a Twitter chat: a Twitter account (duh) and a completed bio. That's it. You did Exercise 12, right?

Finding a Twitter Chat

Once you have the basics in place, you're ready to go. The next step is to find a chat. Chances are good, no matter what the topic is, there's a Twitter chat already out there for you. If there's not, I recommend picking up a copy of Madalyn Sklar's course and starting one yourself.

There are multiple options for finding a Twitter chat. The easiest method is using the search feature in Twitter and typing in your keywords. You'll know you've found one when you see a stream of tweets all using the same hashtag.

You can also do a Google search for "Twitter chats on [insert your keyword]." Other places you can look to find a chat include the following:

1. Twubs.com
2. Tweetchat.com
3. Tweetreports.com
4. Hashtags.org

I also recommend scrolling through the Twitter feed of a few influencers in your area of expertise. Chances are high that if there's a chat about your subject matter, they'll be participating in it, if not hosting it.

You've found a Twitter chat aligned with your keywords and what you want to be known for. You have your bio set up, and you're ready to go. Now what?

It's All about the Hashtag

The hashtag is key in a Twitter chat. In fact, without the hashtag you can't have a Twitter chat. Referring to her Twitter chat, #TwitterSmarter, Madalyn Sklar knows from experience that the biggest learning curve you'll experience with Twitter chats is "remembering to put the hashtag into the tweet. If you don't put the hashtag in your tweet, then we don't see you in the conversation. The conversation revolves around the hashtag."

Notice she said "conversation"? The hashtag is your friend in a Twitter chat. It's what holds the conversation together because, without it your comments will not be included in the chat. So don't forget the hashtag.

Quick note here: You will forget the hashtag. I do it at least once during every chat I participate in. So when you do, don't sweat it. You can simply copy and paste the tweet without the hashtag into a new tweet *with* the hashtag. Or, if no one has re-tweeted or liked your tweet, you can just edit it. Either way, don't worry. It happens to the best of us.

Twitter Chat Structure

Twitter chats begin at the top of the hour. Typically the first five minutes or so of every chat is reserved for introductions and exchanging pleasantries. The host may also post the rules of the chat during this time. Pay attention to these rules. Most hosts I know are sticklers about the rules. They don't tolerate Askholes, and they welcome Relentless Givers.

After the initial introduction the host will post the first question. Once the question is posted, participants respond with their best advice, insight, and opinions using the chat's hashtag.

Twitter chats are fast-paced. Depending on the number of active participants, the tweets can fill up your screen very quickly. For this reason, I recommend that, when you're getting started with Twitter chats, just "listen in." Read the questions and the other participant's responses rather than responding immediately. This is called lurking. You're a participant in the background who is merely paying attention to the chat. There is nothing wrong with being a lurker. In fact, you can glean some great insights about both the participants and the topic just by sitting back and reading the stream of Tweets.

Lurking is a great way to get started, but if you want to build your brand and boost your CareerKred, at some point you'll need to become an active participant. So, when you're ready, jump in with both feet and start answering questions and adding value. Demonstrate your expertise while being a Relentless Giver.

Expect questions to come from the host every six to ten minutes. The timing and the quantity of questions in a chat depend on the amount of participation and the host. Some hosts are pretty rigorous in how they manage a chat, while others are a little more flexible.

Depending on how fast you type, it's highly possible that a new question will be asked before you can bang out an answer to the previous question. If that happens, simply scroll back through the feed to read the new question and see the responses from others.

Twitter Chat Attendees

If you're concerned about not being the "right fit" for a chat, start by being a lurker. Listen in first, and then participate. Keep in mind that a typical Twitter chat will have a variety of attendees from different disciplines, all of whom share the same or similar interests.

Mark Babbitt's Twitter chat (#Internpro), for example, sees "a good mix of experts in the career space, so a chat might include resume writers, recruiters, career coaches, and those looking for a job or an internship."

Regardless of your current level of expertise in your subject area, every Twitter chat will have people who are one step or more above you and people who are one step or more below your level of expertise. That's the beauty of a Twitter chat, and that's why I recommend them to everyone. There is such a huge breadth of experiences and insights in every chat that you are guaranteed to learn something. Remember, chats are peer-to-peer masterminds with like-minded people.

When you actively participate, you not only share your wisdom and experiences, but you demonstrate your expertise in a way that is not "bragging" or self-inflating. You're sharing in the spirit of being a Relentless Giver, which will encourage others to see you as an expert.

Here's the thing about Twitter chats, and really, there's no way around it: The best way to learn about them is to find one and participate. There are a few other nuances about chats I've left out, but nothing you won't pick up on very quickly once you're in a chat.

Exercise 20—Participate in a Twitter Chat

Now that you know the value of a Twitter chat for boosting your CareerKred, and you know the basics of how to participate, you've got no excuse to not participate in one.

Head over to Twitter and conduct a search starting with your keywords and using a hashtag in front of them. Chances are good you'll find one. Once you know the time and date, get on Twitter and start tweeting.

Here are four ways to find a Twitter chat:

- Twubs.com
- Tweetchat.com
- Hashtags.org
- Tweetreports.com/twitter-chat-schedule

Here is a list of my favorite Twitter chats to get you started. Even if the topic is outside of your area of expertise, these chats are very well run and will help you get a feel for how they work.

- #TwitterSmarter—Hosted by @MadalynSkylar. Thursdays at 1:00 p.m. EST. All things Twitter.
- #Internpro—Hosted by @Youtern. Monday at 8:00 p.m. EST. All things career.
- #blogelevated—Hosted by @blogelevated. Monday at 9:00 p.m. EST. All things blogging.
- #brandchat—Hosted by @mariaduron. Wednesdays at 11:00 a.m. EST. All things branding.

Twitter chats are a great way for you to expand your reach beyond your normal following. So be sure to take advantage of this excellent method for networking, audience building, and CareerKred boosting. Happy Tweeting!

Chapter 42

Get Active on LinkedIn

I'm often asked why I recommend starting with both LinkedIn and Twitter. It's simple: Twitter and LinkedIn are a perfect complement to each other. You find people on LinkedIn you want to reach out to, and then head to Twitter to start a conversation.

You can do this the other way as well—you can find people on Twitter and then head to LinkedIn, but generally speaking LinkedIn is not the conversational platform Twitter has become. When working with clients, I always recommend that they use LinkedIn to find people in their niche. It's easier, and it's what LinkedIn was designed to do.

This is not to say that you cannot hold a conversation a on LinkedIn. You can, but you just have to go about it in a different way. Let's spend a few minutes discussing how you can use LinkedIn to start conversations and engage with other business professionals.

LinkedIn Pulse

LinkedIn has tried for years to become the go-to place for business professionals. And while most business professionals have a LinkedIn profile, what LinkedIn really wanted was to become the place where professionals published and consumed content related to their industries. This is why LinkedIn acquired Pulse in 2013.

With Pulse, LinkedIn took a big step forward toward meeting this goal. Pulse allows users to not only publish their own content but also to share and comment on the content of others.

LinkedIn as a professional network is where the business professionals hang. Pulse allows you to demonstrate your expertise, but at the same time it allows you to be a Relentless Giver. Two birds. One stone.

Publish Content on Pulse

Similar to the blog on your website, Pulse allows you to post content related to your area of expertise directly on LinkedIn. This provides you with the potential for your post to be read by other business professionals. If you're just starting out, it allows you to put your content in front of an audience you may not have yet developed.

Also like your blog, publishing regularly gives people a reason to come back to your profile and read about your thoughts on a particular topic. You're putting yourself out there and potentially helping others in the process. It's the perfect way to demonstrate your expertise while helping others and not "tooting your own horn."

Posting your thoughts on your area of expertise via LinkedIn Pulse will have the added benefit of helping others get to know and like you. Do it enough, and they will start to trust you. From an employer or potential employer's standpoint, putting your thoughts out there will also help them assess you for cultural fit and potential opportunities.

Share Content

In addition to publishing content, LinkedIn also allows you to share content on its platform. Updates are LinkedIn's way of allowing its users to curate content on its platform.

In case you were wondering, the difference between an update and a post is simple. An update is you sharing the content usually created by others (i.e, content curation). A post is you sharing the content you create for others.

So, if you find an article you feel will be of interest to your audience or network, feel free to share it via Updates on LinkedIn. Keep in mind however, that LinkedIn is a business professionals network. It is not Facebook, as we discussed earlier. Do not share pictures of your pets or your vacation. Stay professional and on brand at all times.

Like Content on Pulse

When you read a good article someone has shared on LinkedIn, click the Like button below the post. This is does a couple of things for you. First, it almost guarantees that the person who posted the article will notice you have liked it.

Second, a notification is sent to your followers on the platform telling them that you liked an update. This allows for the update to potentially be shared with a larger audience, assuming, of course, that your audience takes the time to click through to see what you liked.

Liking content on LinkedIn is a good way to get yourself noticed by others outside of your network. Your second- and third-degree connections or your weak connections may decide to review your profile and connect after you've liked a particular post. After all, they were reading the post for a reason similar to yours.

Comment on Content on Pulse

Commenting on a post or update within LinkedIn is a great way to invite people into a conversation. This is true in general, but especially on LinkedIn, since seemingly people are more reluctant to converse on the platform than on other platforms.

When commenting on an post or update, make your comment genuine and thoughtful. Just saying something like "Great post" doesn't really invite others to chime in. Instead take the time to compose a two- to three-sentence response to the post and offer some insights or observations on the topic that are your own. Doing this will make your comment stand out while inviting others to join in.

Another benefit of commenting is that you can do it in the spirit of the Relentless Giver by crafting your comment so it includes an example from your experiences that may help educate someone else who has not had the same experiences. In this case, everybody wins.

Introduce People to Your Network

The key to using LinkedIn is to continue to build your professional network while maintaining the Relentless Giver mindset. Publishing posts, updates, liking, commenting, and curating content are all great ways to extend your brand while providing useful information to others. Another great way to use LinkedIn is to introduce people in your network to others.

Giving credit where it is due, I first learned about this during a webinar hosted by Trevor Young. Trevor follows a person named Darrel Griffin. Darrel is a LinkedIn mentor and profile writer as well as a signage and digital print adviser.

What's so interesting about Darrel? Well, Darrel uses his platform on LinkedIn to introduce people in his network to other people in his network via the publishing feature. How cool is that?

I want to dissect this approach because it's very unique, and I personally think it's brilliant. What a great way to share someone else's unique gifts and talents with others! By doing this, Darrel is providing others with the opportunity to discover someone else—to potentially make a new weak connection.

If that weak connection happens to be someone who offers assistance with that "thing" you've been struggling with, well, you might just have found an answer to your challenge in this person. While I personally do not know Darrel, this effort alone tells me a lot about him and his Relentless Giver mindset. My personal hope is that his example is picked up and followed by others. You never know whom you might meet following Darrel's example.

Exercise 21—Get Active on LinkedIn

Regardless of your past experience with the platform, now is the time in your brand-building journey to embrace LinkedIn as it was originally intended: as a way to build your professional network. This week, if not today, take the time to complete any of the following activities on LinkedIn:

- Publish a post on Pulse
- Like a post
- Comment on a post
- Share a post

If you're up to a challenge, take a few minutes and introduce someone in your network to others in your network. You never know what good may come from it.

Engage Step 3

Chapter 43

Expand Your Reach

The entire Engage step is based around engaging with your audience, or as Trevor Young likes to say, "pressing the flesh." While a slang term typically reserved for politicians who get out from behind a podium and shake the hands of their followers, "pressing the flesh" is a good metaphor for the Engage step.

In today's digital age, you can press the flesh both in person and digitally to continue to grow your network. As you can imagine, there are a multitude of ways in which you can do this, and the methods you choose should be the ones that work best for you.

Engagement is all about carrying on the conversations you've already started as well as starting new ones. And before you tell me you're an introvert and you don't like to talk to other people, stop for a minute and look at how far you've come.

If you've been completing the exercises in the book, you've defined your brand. You've integrated it online, which is a huge step that most people won't do. You've started to create content and put yourself out there in a way you may have never thought possible. It's only natural at this point for you to continue what you started by continuing to push the limits of your comfort zone.

The secret to doing the Engage step properly is to always be networking. As I said earlier, this is the essence of the Engage step. With this mind, here are some other methods you can use to continue to engage with your audience as well as continue to expand your network beyond Twitter and LinkedIn.

Commenting on Blog Posts

Commenting on the blog posts of others is a hidden secret to building your brand. Commenting affords you with three benefits: First, you capture the attention of the post author; second, you can demonstrate your expertise and Relentless Giver mindset by adding more value to the post; and finally, when you comment on a post as yourself, you usually include a link back to your site.

As a blogger, I can tell you that there is no better way to grab my attention than to leave a comment on one of my posts. Good or bad, I will notice. If you leave an insightful comment, not only will I take note, but I will most likely respond to you as well.

Once I've responded, what I've really done is open the door for further conversations with you. Take advantage of this by heading over to Twitter and following the author of the post there. If he or she follows you back, again it's an invitation for further conversations. Just remember, conversation, *not* conversion.

If you comment on a network like Disqus, which is a blog comment-hosting service for websites and online communities, all of your comments will be captured by the system. Anyone else using Disqus can easily go through all of your comments online.

If your comments add value and are aligned around what you want to be known for, people will very quickly pick up on this and begin to perceive you in that light. That's why we talked about congruency—it even applies to your comments online.

Quora

Quora falls along the same lines as commenting on blogs, with a difference: It's a question-and-answer website. Quora users post questions about a specific topic, and other Quora members provide answers. You see where I'm going with this, right?

Quora was founded in June 2009 and made available to the public on June 21, 2010. Its purpose is to develop communities and thought leadership around topics, questions, and answers. It's a great way for you to boost your CareerKred.

Like a Twitter chat, Quora allows you to demonstrate your expertise without being perceived as arrogant, pompous, or an Askhole. It gives you the opportunity to be a Relentless Giver.

Once you create your Quora account, you can answer any questions on the site, but I advise against that. Unless you have an answer to a question that involves you solving someone's issue, I suggest you resist the temptation to answer any questions outside of what you want to be known for. Instead, stay congruent and only answer questions related to the keywords selected in Exercise 17.

Here's another secret about Quora: It's great for generating ideas for blog posts. Remember, if people are posting questions, they are legitimately seeking answers. By answering their questions with your knowledge and expertise, you are helping them out, but if you notice a lot of people answering a question, that means people have opinions about it, so it must be a hot topic.

Here's a list of questions I found using the keyword "personal branding":

1. What are your thoughts on personal blog names?
2. What are the best tools to use in personal branding?
3. What are some of the top tools for brand-reputation management?
4. How can I improve my personal brand as project manager over the Internet?
5. What are some of the best LinkedIn profile headlines?
6. How do you brand yourself online?

As you might guess, I like the last the question best. Take a minute and read through these questions. Can you see how answering them with your knowledge and pointing the questioners to resources on the Web can quickly position you as someone who understands the topic very well? Remember the shoe salesperson from earlier?

In addition, you can use the exact question to create a longer answer as a blog post. Example: How do you brand yourself online? Use the DICE process, of course.

Attending Conferences

When was the last time you attended a conference?

As I began this journey several years, one of things I decided to do was attend my first conference. Immediately afterward I started to realize the power of attending a conference when it comes to building your network.

I met people at that first conference who inspired and motivated me. Conferences are a great place to foster your network of weak connections. Madalyn Sklar agrees. She personally goes to conferences in order to "meet people she would not otherwise have the opportunity to meet."

This past summer, for example, I attended the Gallup Strengths Conference. While there, I was introduced a person who definitely operated outside of my sphere of knowledge. We talked for no more than ten minutes, exchanged contact information, and moved on. I'm not sure either of us thought much about the conversation immediately afterward.

A month later, however, this person did the one thing Madalyn recommends when you meet people at a conference—he followed up. He sent me an email asking if we could talk further. We scheduled a time to talk and realized we had opportunities to collaborate. He is now my number-one referrer for new business, and our weak connection has grown to a strong one.

I make a point to attend at least one conference every year. Conferences have become an important part of my annual learning plan. I realize conferences can be costly, but if you select the right one, it can pay for itself via your new network of weak connections.

Attending Meet Ups

Meet ups are a less-costly version of a conference. They are held in your local area and hosted by local residents. Meet ups are very niche-oriented, so the attendees are almost guaranteed to be of a similar mind to your own. This is a great way to meet new weak connections.

A host schedules meet ups. The host can be anyone—*you* can be a host. The only requirements to being a host are taking the initiative to schedule the meeting and promoting it. Being a meet-up host is a great way to be seen as an authority in your niche while providing a boost to your CareerKred in the attendees' eyes.

To find or schedule a meet up, go to meetup.com. Before you schedule a new meet up, do a quick search using your keywords to see if there are already meet ups in your area. If there are, join the group, and you'll be notified when the next meet up gets scheduled.

Alternatively, if you can't find a preexisting meet up, consider starting your own. Yes, it involves effort on your part, but the connections you make will more than likely out weigh your efforts.

The Engage Step Checklist

- [ ] Take the Digital Brand Assessment (if not already completed)
- [ ] Score: _______________

Step #1 - Network Like Rock Star

- [ ] Identify times in the past week where you engaged in networking
- [ ] Establish your networking goals
- [ ] Identify who you should network with
- [ ] Develop your connection strategy
- [ ] Setup your curation workflow

Step #2 - Using Social Media

- [ ] Identify and participate in a Twitter chat
- [ ] Get involved on LinkedIn. Like, comment, share and post an article using Pulse

Step #3 - Expand your reach

- [ ] Comment on an influencer or industry blog post
- [ ] Answer a question on Quora
- [ ] Identify a conference to attend
- [ ] Identify and attend a Meetup in your area

Part Seven

Wrap

"You're afraid of change. I don't know the future.
I didn't come here to tell you how this is going to end.
I came here to show you how it's going to begin."
—Neo

Chapter 44

Do You Believe in Fate?

One of my favorite scenes from the movie *The Matrix* is called "The Pill." I think it makes the perfect metaphor to describe where you are now as you reach the end of this book.

At the heart of this scene, Morpheus presents Thomas Anderson with a choice. This choice becomes his inciting incident. Maybe you remember the scene: Red pill or blue pill? One pill allows him to continue to live in the fictional, computer-generated world, the only world he has ever known. The other pill allows him to embrace a new path by joining the "real world" and escaping from the Matrix.

During the scene, Morpheus talks to Thomas about the feelings he has been wrestling with. You see, Thomas has felt for a long time that there is something more out there for him. Perhaps, like Thomas, you experience similar feelings and struggle to explain them.

My guess is that you probably can't pinpoint the origin of your feelings, either. Maybe they started after you were turned down for a promotion. Maybe you feel you are not recognized for your expertise. Or maybe you've just been in the same role, industry, or career for so long that you ache to do something different.

No matter what feelings lead you to this point, you are here now, and our paths have crossed for a reason. Now that you are at the end of this book, you've arrived at your "red pill, blue pill" moment, so to speak—your inciting incident.

At the beginning of the scene, Morpheus asks Thomas if he believes in fate. He answers no, "because I don't like the idea that I'm not in control of my life."

Maybe you feel the same way. On the one hand, the blue pill signifies that you believe reading this book at this point in your career was inevitable, a path predetermined by forces beyond your control.

On the other hand, the red pill tells you that there are no predetermined paths for your life and career. You have arrived at this point by choice—your choice—by following the path you have created or are seeking to create for yourself.

Many people, perhaps even you, have been progressing through their careers because they know no other way. It's the path determined by the blue pill. Unfortunately for us, the reality is that the blue pill world of work you are used to is quickly fading. Dorie Clark reminded me of that when she told me: "Standing out is no longer an option." If you want the opportunities of the future to turn toward you, you need to make sure the opportunities can see you—that you stand out in the sea of sameness.

Following the blue pill, old-school career formula of "go to school, get good grades, and live happily ever after" doesn't work anymore. You have to adopt a new way. The DICE process outlined in this book is the different way. It's your red pill.

Unfortunately, like the matrix itself, despite my best efforts to lay out the steps in this book, "No one can be told what the matrix is; you have to see it for yourself." Some of you will choose the blue pill. It's safe and comforting, and let's face it, you have it pretty good, don't you? My guess is you do—at least until you don't.

Like Morpheus told the soon-to-become Neo, "All I'm offering you is the truth. Nothing more." The world of work you know will exist in the future for some of you, but not for all. As technology continues to replace job functions that were once deemed sacred, if you are to escape the career matrix, you must improvise, adapt, and overcome.

The Impact of Artificial Intelligence

At the time of this writing, artificial intelligence is gaining traction and will increase exponentially over the coming years. We see it in our phones with Siri, Cortana, Alexa, and OK Google. While still needing much work, these operating systems and the companies that create them are rapidly moving us to what has been called the "Robot Economy."

An article from *Business Insider* written in 2013 by Max Nisen started with the title "Robot Economy Could Cause up to 75 Percent Unemployment."[15] While this may seem ridiculous to you, in this article Mr. Nisen explains that smarter computers will eventually replace jobs that involve a standard routine.

In the same article, Martin Ford, a software entrepreneur, stated: "The vast majority of people do routine work, because the human economy has always demanded routine work." Consider your current role for a minute. Do you engage in routine work?

Before you answer, consider these two examples. It's estimated that pilots only actively steer an airplane for three to seven minutes for most flights. The rest of the flight is done via autopilot. Think about the driverless cars Google and Uber are researching. Both of these examples on the surface appear to be very complex activities, yet at their core they are governed by standard routines.

Think back to the beginning of this book and the story of Max the Accountant. Accounting is filled with standard routines; in fact, it's governed by them via the generally accepted accounting principles known as GAAP.

If you look up GAAP on Google, you'll find this definition: "Generally accepted accounting principles is a term used to refer to the accounting standards used in any given jurisdiction." Accounting standards equal routines. Think about the application of AI to the routines or standard work practices in this case, and it's easy to see why poor Max never saw this coming.

In November 2015 the *McKinsey Quarterly* published an article titled "Four Fundamentals of Workplace Automation." In this article, the author's research suggests that "as many as 45 percent of the activities individuals are paid to perform can be automated by adapting currently demonstrated technologies."[16]

And before you try to rationalize between white-collar and blue-collar roles, the article goes on to say that an estimated "20 percent of a CEO's working time could be automated."

---

15 Nisen, M. (2013) Robot economy could cause up to 75 percent unemployment. Retrieved from http://www.businessinsider.com/50-percent-unemployment-robot-economy-2013-1.

16 Chui, M. & Manyika, J. & Miremandi, M. (2015) Four fundamentals of workplace automation. Retrieved from http://www.mckinsey.com/business-functions/digital-mckinsey/our-insights/four-fundamentals-of-workplace-automation.

I'm not sharing these articles and statistics to scare you. I share them to help you to, as Morpheus would say, "open your mind." Open your mind to the possibilities. Open your mind and explore where your career is taking you now versus where it could take you if you decide to roll the DICE.

While I'm not asking you to escape the Matrix, I am asking you to make a choice today. I don't want you to arrive at work someday only to discover the choice has been made for you. I've seen it happen to others. I don't want it to happen to you.

So what will it be for you? Red pill or blue pill?

In closing, consider this. There is no perfect time or perfect content, and there is no day on your calendar called "someday." While following the predetermined path (blue pill) is easier, it leaves you largely not in control of your own fate.

The career landscape is changing. Technology will only accelerate these changes. This is why starting a new path now is much better than trying to wait it out.

Following the DICE process will boost your CareerKred, but it's not a quick win. Rather, it's a long-term, ongoing activity, so don't wait to be perfect to get started. When it comes to your CareerKred, it truly doesn't matter where you start.

What does matter is where you end up.

As the author, my hope is that you choose, or have already chosen, the red pill. If you have, say it with me one more time.

"I am a brand."

About the Author

Ryan Rhoten is a marketing and branding guide. He founded CareerBrand Inc., a branding agency for career coaches and business professionals, to help them boost their CareerKred by extend-ing their brands into the online space.

Using a simple four-step process he created called DICE, Ryan helps coaches build digital trust with their clients by providing them with clarity in their branding, positioning, and marketing methods. Ryan's process has been featured on various podcasts and online publications, including *Forbes* and *Mashable*.

At CareerBrand, Ryan is an author, blogger, speaker, executive personal-brand mentor, and the host of the popular iTunes podcast, *The BRAND New You Show*. Through his podcast, Ryan has interviewed over seventy- five personal brand and social media experts as well as career coaches, recruiters, and talent management professionals.

Looking for Help Implementing Your Digital Brand Online?

If you are interested in hiring Ryan to help build your digital brand, whether business or personal, there are a variety of ways you can work with him.

Speaking engagements

Ryan is available for a variety of presentations and breakout sessions on all the topics covered in this book:

- Unpacking your process to unlock your brand's potential
- Leveraging your digital brand to build your CareerKred
- Build your personal brand digitally in four simple steps
- Creating your executive, C-Suite, and CEO brand
- Accelerate your content production using the Content Pyramid

Unpack your process

This is a one-on-one, one-hour session where Ryan will guide you through unpacking your coaching process step-by-step. Once completed, Ryan will "reassemble" your process visually in order to provide you with a brandable and marketable coaching method you can use to provide clarity to your clients. In addition, Ryan will also show you how you can leverage your process to create lead magnets, eBooks, marketing funnels, an online course outline, and a content schedule so you never need to worry about what to post again.

CareerKred Assessment

This one-hour, lightning-round session is for individuals and small business brands where Ryan will personally help you assess where your brand stands today and the key next-step actions you need to take in order to boost your CareerKred and build your digital brand. During the call Ryan will assess your online and social media presence, and the call will conclude with Ryan's findings and recommendations.

Boost Your CareerKred

This is a four-month program. Ryan will personally work with you one-on-one and serve as your brand manager to help you design and implement a digital branding strategy just for you following the steps in the DICE process. This is the ultimate CareerKred boosting package for executives who understand the importance of establishing their online presence, their thought leadership, and their overall digital brand as it relates to their career.

Digital Branding Package for Small Business and Coaches

Many coaches and small business owners Ryan works with suffer from two things: the "curse of knowledge" and being busy beyond belief. In this three- to six-month program, Ryan will provide you with both front-end and back-end consultation and the implementation you need to get your brand recognized. The program is tailored to meet your needs and could include content identification, content repurposing, lead magnet and sales funnels set up, podcast set up, email marketing, and inbound marketing services.

84015525R00166

Made in the USA
San Bernardino, CA
05 August 2018